Pre-Publication Reviews

"This is a fascinating book! Each of its four authors is an accomplished scholar in the area of moral rights, especially its very complex subdomain of human rights. From their different perspectives they clarify the ongoing, socially constructed character of rights theory in general as well as its specific but elusive contemporary version, "human rights." After a very useful introduction, the first essay, by P. Werhane and T. Wren, fits the philosophical discourse of moral rights neatly into the larger context of social construction theory, showing that "rights talk" is an ongoing, continually developing phenomenon, one that continues to develop as the forces of globalization change our moral perspectives on human rights. The second essay, by the education scholar M. Bellino, describes the various "narratives" on human rights that shape the postwar discourse of young Guatemalans who are now trying to reconstruct for themselves the horrific human rights abuses of their long civil war. It is followed by a careful, painstaking critique by D. Ozar of the controversial notion of "manifesto rights," which are rights that are not correlated with anyone's actual duties toward distant others. The final essay, also by Wren, uses social construction theory to trace the emergence of our notion of a personal "right" from the ancient Greek and Roman idea of "rightness." All in all, this is a very sophisticated yet quite readable contribution to the ongoing discussion of moral rights in general and human rights in particular. It is, in short, a "must read" for anyone interested in these issues."
—Dennis J. McGuire, PhD, Author of *Healing the Wounds of Childhood.*

Human Rights and Cultural Meanings

Human Rights and Cultural Meanings

The Social Construction of Classical and Contemporary Rights Talk

Thomas E. Wren, Editor

New University Press LLC

Los Angeles • Las Vegas

New University Press LLC
5013 Range View Avenue
Los Angeles, CA 90042

For permissions, contact
info@newuniversitypress.com

Cover by Trescela Samson

Acknowledgment: Reformatted with minor editing, and reprinted with permission from the editors of *Listening: Journal of Communication Ethics, Religion, and Culture.* Fall, 2014

ISBN: 978-0-9829219-6-8

Library of Congress Control Number: 2015943538

BISAC Codes:
PHI005000 Philosophy/Ethics & Moral Philosophy
POL035010 Political Science/Human Rights

Contents

1

Introduction

Thomas E. Wren

Today rights talk is everywhere. It is spoken by social activists, politicians and policy wonks, practicing lawyers and legal theorists, victims of structural injustices such as racism, sexism, homophobia, and of course by moral philosophers and educators. Much, perhaps most, of that discourse takes place within relatively tight social and intellectual circles, but there is also considerable crosstalk and leakage between them. At first sight the classical and contemporary scholarly literature about moral rights, including the important subdomain of human rights, seems rigorously analytic, fine-grained, and often intimidating in its historical sweep. However, a closer look reveals that this literature is actually a surprisingly diverse collection—jumble might be better term—of motifs, suppositions, logical implications, and ad hoc *pronunciamientos* about the various rights and duties we have toward each other. In this short introduction I will sketch why this is so, as well as why the wide conceptual diversity of rights talk is a very good thing. In doing so, I will refer to the rich history of rights discourse, not in order to referee the various classical and contemporary debates about rights and duties but only to acknowledge that to understand those issues properly, one must appreciate the socially constructed character of the classical and contemporary rights literature.

In his curiously titled book *The Social Construction of What?* the Canadian philosopher Ian Hacking has introduced the metaphor of a matrix to describe how ideas are socially constructed.[1] "Ideas do not exist in a vacuum," he said. "They inhabit a social setting. Let us call that the matrix within which an idea, a concept or kind, is formed. 'Matrix' is no more perfect for my purpose than the word 'idea,'" Hacking admitted, and then explained that the term is derived from the word for womb. At the heart of this interesting maternal metaphor is the idea that social construction is a discursive process in which concepts such as "race," "gender," "culture," and now "rights" are created and shaped (and recreated and reshaped). But what is this mysterious process, and how does it work in the case of moral rights?

My own admittedly very general and nontechnical answer to this question has four parts or dimensions.[2] Concepts like those just mentioned are constructed through (1) formal and informal conversations that have (2) ever-changing vocabularies, as well as multiple but not always distinct (3) levels of social prestige, intimacy, institutional structure, and intellectual complexity, and (4) specific issues or conflicts that give rise to the discourse in the first place. For instance, rights talk has always been at least implicitly conversational, not only in the academic sense of learned theoretical dialogues and formal debates but also in the pragmatic sense of interested parties negotiating an acceptable balance of burdens and benefits. As for the vocabulary of rights talk, it seems safe to say that in its earlier, more theoretical moments, discourse about rights and duties was heavily metaphysical and even theological, but it is now much more legalistic and case oriented. As for its levels, there have probably always been differences in the levels of sophistication and social positions of the participants, even though scholarly accounts of the historical development of rights theory are based almost exclusively on the writings of a relatively small number of established intellectuals such as William of Ockham,[3] John Locke, J.-J. Rousseau, Immanuel Kant, and the authors of the American and French Declarations. Exactly what the ordinary folk of those and earlier eras were thinking and saying to each other about their mutual obligations can only be inferred from documents written by their literate, relatively well-educated, and politically influential contemporaries. Fortunately, we are better informed about the everyday discourse of the last two or three centuries. Thanks to developments in the popular media since the late 1700s, historians and social theorists have been able to track (or reconstruct) many of the moral discourse patterns of the general populace.[4] As for the specific issues or conflicts that have been addressed in rights talk, it is relatively easy to identify significant historical shifts, including both short and long term changes in public discourse. For instance it is quite clear that sometime over the last decade or two "Human Rights" became a verbal banner under which gay activists chose to march. It has also served as the banner for women's issues over the last several decades, and before then it was invoked in struggles against such large-scale evils as racism, genocide, political oppression, poverty, and famine.[5] The list is long and all-too-familiar. Indeed, it may be hard to believe that the very notion of rights is a relatively late development in the history of moral and legal discourse.

About This Volume

Of the four "Rights" chapters in this volume, the first one, "Human Rights as Social Constructions" by Patricia Werhane and myself, is the most directly focused on the socially constructed character of the concept of rights, especially the contemporary notion of human rights. A case in point is the recent work of the Oxford philosopher James Griffin, who has been unusually frank about the adventitious character of even the most (supposedly) systematic accounts of human rights, including his own will- or agency-based account as well as the more familiar interest-based accounts that are identified with earlier twentieth-century philosophers such as Henry Shue and Ronald Dworkin. We conclude that abstract models of human rights, including Griffin's (we think he would agree), are not eternal truths but rather historical phenomena that provide more or less useful conceptual schemes for generating universally (or almost universally) acceptable principles of fairness, liberty, mutual respect, security, and so on. This bottom-up constructionist approach encourages such dialogues despite the improbability of full consensus and yet without denying that there could be a set of general normative principles that all peoples would find acceptable.

The inherently unfinished character of human rights discourse is illustrated in a different way by Michelle

Bellino's remarkable ethnographic study of the recep-
tion by Guatemalan school children and young adults of
a human rights educational program that was set up in
the aftermath of their country's horrific 36-year civil
war. She presents a graphic typology of human rights
consciousness, based on fourteen months of fieldwork,
in which teenagers and young adults exhibit three
sharply contrasting narrative stances toward the past
and present violence of their society: narratives of denial
in which adolescents reject the normative claims of the
human rights framework, narratives of skepticism in
which they question whether human rights can be effectively practiced in Guatemala, and narratives of empowerment in which they understand justice initiatives for
past and present violence through the lens of human
rights. In general they are underwhelmed by the international rhetoric of human rights and democracy, often
regarding it as camouflage for past and present atroci-
ties on both sides of the conflict. As an educator, Bellino
questions whether the curricular reforms associated
with postwar policies (a) are effective at achieving their
intended goals of fostering informed and engaged civic
attitudes and actions, (b) carry the same civic potential
when disarticulated from coverage of recent conflict, (c)
are interpreted as valuable and valid stances by students
and members of civil society, and (d) are actively cri-
tiqued in informal learning contexts.

The third chapter, David Ozar's "Human Rights and
the Rest of Us," also focuses on human rights theory,
this time using the surgical tools of contemporary ana-
lytical philosophy rather than real-life narratives and
case studies. His point of departure is the late Joel
Feinberg's well-known assertion in the wake of the UN
Declaration that human rights claims, including the
right to life itself, are "manifestos" addressed to everyone in principle and no one in particular. In this view

(which Ozar rejects) there is no direct coupling of rights and duties such as those we find in more specific correlations of rights and duties, such as workers' rights to compensation from their employers or parents' duties to provide appropriate sustenance to their children. Because of the indeterminate target of human rights claims, Feinberg and others who have followed his lead have diluted the notion of human rights to what he calls "manifesto rights," which are the responsibilities of governments and international agencies but not, except in very special circumstances, requirements placed on private individuals. Ozar rejects this view, drawing on more recent philosophical literature such as Henry Shue's notion of "basic rights" to show that human rights do indeed generate moral imperatives for all of us, even though sorting out just who has which duties and how they should be fulfilled are questions that are often extraordinarily difficult to resolve either in theory or in practice. In the course of examining and charitably reconstructing Feinberg's original position in terms of more recent human rights models, Ozar demonstrates that at least in some general sense the human rights claims of distant others are addressed to all of us, albeit in many different ways.

The final chapter, my own "The Birth of Rights Talk," is rather different than the others, but it provides a useful historical context within which the essentially constructed character of rights discourse can be understood. Here the central issue is not what might be called the logical geography of our current conceptions of moral rights but rather the historical transition from the classical notion of objective rightness to the modern notion of rights as powers. No Greek, Roman, or early medieval speaker ever said "I have a right," but it was commonplace for their philosophers, jurists, and other intellectuals to insist that there was "a right way" of doing things, which is to say a more or less obvious natural order that could be read off from their respective historical records. Exactly when the idea of "the right way" mutated into the concept of a personal or collective right is still a contested issue, but as I have shown, there is good reason to think that the transformation took place in the high middle ages, as part of a larger social transformation that included new modes of discourse, interpretations of sacred and classical texts, and yes, rough and ready litigating. If my account is basically correct (and it probably is, since it reflects the consensus of classical and medieval scholars over the last several decades), its implication for contemporary rights theory is obvious: there are new conceptions (or sets of conceptions) of moral and political rights out there, waiting, like the rough beast of Yeats' poem, to be born. Whether that is good news or bad news remains to be seen, but in either case it provides the perspective from which the essays in this volume should be read.[6]

Notes

1. Ian Hacking, *The Social Construction of What?* (Cambridge: Harvard University Press, 1999), 10. Hacking's metaphor is discussed at greater length below, in Werhane and Wren's contribution to this volume.
2. In developing these ideas I have drawn on discussions of discourse theory by communication theorists such as Michael Billig, *Arguing and Thinking* (Cambridge: Cambridge University Press, 1996), as well as the philosopher Rom Harré's "ethogenic" approach to social phenomena; see his *Social Being* (Oxford: Blackwell, 1979). See also his "An Ontology for Duties and Rights," in *The Psychology of Rights and Duties: Empirical Contributions and Normative Commentaries,* ed. N.

Finkel and F. Moghaddam (Washington, DC: American Psychological Association, 2008), 223-41.

3. Though not Aristotle or Thomas Aquinas, as I will show in my own contribution to this volume.

4. For some of the best discussions of this important point see Benedict Anderson, *Imagined Communities: Reflections on the Origin and Spread of Nationalism* (London: Verso, 1991); Mary Poovey, *Making a Social Body* (Chicago: University of Chicago Press, 1998); and Charles Taylor, *Modern Social Imaginaries* (Durham, NC: Duke University Press, 2004).

5. The term "human rights" calls to mind Tom Paine's *Rights of Man*, which was said to have sold over 250,000 copies after it came out in 1791, the same year that the French *Declaration* (after which Paine's book was named) appeared. The gender-neutral term "human rights" did not catch on until it was used as the title of the United Nations Declaration in 1948.

6. Earlier versions of these chapters were published in the Fall 2014 edition of *Listening: Journal of Communication Ethics, Religion, and Culture,* and appear here with the gracious permission of the editors of that journal.

2

Human Rights as Social Constructions

Patricia H. Werhane and Thomas E. Wren

In the following pages we join the ongoing conversation among philosophers, legal and political theorists, humanitarians, and other sorts of globalists concerning the form, content, and use of the general concept of human rights—or better, its family of forms, contents, and uses.[1] In this article we lay out what might be called the forensic (i.e., debate oriented) epistemology or, more plainly, the social constructionist approach that we believe is a fruitful way to understand a complex socio-politico-legal-philosophical issue such as human rights. Then, once our constructionist approach is clarified, we proceed to the second section, where we discuss in greater detail some of the reasons that the complex and important notion of human rights should be understood as a social construction in the generally accepted sense of that term. We also show how a constructionist approach can meet the important objection that human rights theory seems to be a purely Western invention that has little or no conceptual or moral relevance to Asian, African, and other non-Western peoples. In the third section, we illustrate the conversational or dialogical character of human rights theory by analyzing some of the criticisms and replies that were exchanged in a relatively recent symposium devoted to James Griffin's "agency" approach to human rights. Our conclusion, not surprisingly, is that the social constructionist approach is the best (or least bad) available method for dealing with the complex literature of human rights theory and the social policies that invoke it.

Philosophers in the English-speaking world now generally agree that since the middle of the 20th century the philosophical conversation about rights in general has been shaped by two carefully wrought accounts, namely interest-based accounts on the one hand and will- or agency-based accounts on the other. This parsing also applies to human rights theories but in strikingly different ways, as we will explain momentarily. A third account, which we discuss at length, has also emerged, mainly in the literature of sociology and ethnomethodology but also in important non-mainstream philosophical literatures variously identified with American pragmatism, critical theory, and social constructionism. For all their differences, these various streams often converge.

Turning now to the current philosophical literature about human rights, we should first acknowledge that it includes carefully wrought updates of the classical natural law accounts of rights and duties. Although no longer dominant, naturalistic views are still alive and well, especially in applied contexts such as debates about the permissibility of abortion or torture.[2] However, most of the scholarly reviews of the rights literature that appear in today's philosophy journals, textbooks, and anthologies bundle the contemporary philosophical treatments of rights and human rights under the twin headings of interest theory and will theory, especially the latter's latest version, also called agency theory. A good example of the current conversation about those approaches is the above-mentioned symposium, in which several prominent rights theorists reacted to James Griffin's *On Human Rights*.[3] In section three we track some of the dialectics in play concerning that book and a few other recent exchanges.

While there is general agreement in the current human rights literature on the importance of rights talk, there is by no means any consensus regarding its theoretical bases. This is a long-standing controversy. For example, three years after the appearance of John Rawls's *Theory of Justice* Robert Nozick countered its "fairness" conception of rights with the libertarian thesis that only civil liberties should count as rights, and then only as negative rights, such as the right not to be harmed or interfered with. A few years later, Henry Shue used the distinction between basic and non-basic rights to argue that survival and security are the first priorities because they make all other rights claims possible. David Ozar, in his contribution to this volume, elaborates on that thesis. These and other distinctions and qualifications are part of a rich and ongoing conversation about the nature and content of human rights. It is a debate that is inherently open-ended for the basic reason that—as we will show in the following sections—rights talk is itself a socially constructed phenomenon. If so, there is no reason to expect that the debates over the prioritization, content, and nature of human rights will ever be decisively settled.

A Social Constructionist Approach

Within the vast literature on rights, one finds several sources of confusion or ambiguity, four of which are worth mentioning here. The first is the fact that rights talk is a relatively late development in the history of philosophy. Although threads of thinking about what we now call rights appeared as early as the Stoics if not Aristotle, a full-blown, systematic theory of natural rights did not emerge until the 17th century. Second, non-Western accounts of rights in general and human rights in particular are significant by their absence in the history of philosophy. Whether this absence is the result of deep-seated differences between Western and non-Western notions of the human person—specifically the notion that humans have a privileged place in the universe—remains to be seen. Third, there is an ongoing and perhaps unresolvable debate about which rights are especially important or most fundamental. For example, we saw above that the question is still at issue regarding which is more basic or fundamental: the freedom to make basic choices (the agency-based theory) or survival and physical security (the interest-based theory). Fourth and most important in the present context, there seems to be little prospect of any final resolution of basic philosophical differences on related topics such as the catalog of human rights or the line between absolute and aspirational rights, despite the flood of ink already devoted to such topics.

We suggest, then, a way of thinking about rights that accommodates these internal divisions and ambiguities, namely, to recognize that rights talk is itself a socially constructed phenomenon rather than a rigorously logical set of definitions and inferences. In this section, we will develop that idea, beginning with an explanation of the often undertheorized term "social construction," or as it is sometimes called, "social constructionism."[4] Its starting point is the recognition that we are not passive and solitary thinkers who quietly form mental pictures of our experiences, which is to say mimetic representations that are somehow derived from the stimuli (data) to which we are subjected, and from which all human learning and social interactions result. Rather, our minds continually interact with others as well as with the data of our experiences (most if not all of which are shared), selectively filtering and framing that data though various social learning processes, mind sets, and mental models.[5] In the process of focusing, framing, organizing, ordering, and discussing what we experience, we mentally bracket or simply omit some data because we cannot observe or absorb all that we encounter through perception. To state our view in the language of social epistemology, we believe that knowledge is the product of social and cultural factors as well as natural ones.[6]

It is now generally agreed that although the constitutive interaction between the perceiver and the perceived (which Kant simply called experience) includes physiological processes, it cannot be explained solely in terms of our hard-wiring. Rather, the ways in which we frame, order, and filter our experiences are themselves socially learned and socially exercised. These processes are more or less stable (sometimes more, sometimes less) but always incomplete and hence always revisable. They have been described in various ways: as lenses, perspectives, and frames, or somewhat more abstractly, as conceptual schemes or mental models by which we construct and deconstruct meaning. In sum, they are "mental representations, cognitive frames, or mental pictures through which all human beings perceive and experience, developing incomplete and volatile narratives, observations, and scientific content, all of which is then called 'knowledge.'"[7] In the philosophy of science it is now generally understood that scientific methodologies are themselves mental models or schemes through which scientists discover, predict, and hypothesize about what they then call reality. Social construction theory takes this idea one step further with the claim that our shared mental models or schemes frame all of our experiences in the sense that they guide the ways in which we recognize and organize what we then call the world. From this claim it follows that all realities—or better, all the categories that we apply to reality—are socially structured. Indeed, according to social constructionism, this is the only way in which human beings can understand anything.[8]

Even so, there is a difference between, on the one hand, claiming that one cannot get at reality, or the world, or even experience itself, except through some mental model and, on the other hand, concluding that reality itself is socially constructed. The details of this idea are disputed, but it seems clear that there is a meaningful difference between (1) the contention that the incomplete and disparate ways in which we present and distill experiences are socially constructed and (2) the much more contentious claim that reality itself is socially constructed. Thus Ian Hacking describes a strong or universal constructionist as someone who would argue that every object of knowledge "is in some nontrivial sense socially constructed. Not just our experience of them, our classifications of them, our interests in them, but these things themselves."[9] Or as Nelson Goodman, himself a strong constructionist, famously argued, there are no natural kinds. "If I ask about the world, you can offer to tell me how it is under one or more frames of reference; but if I insist that you tell me how it is apart from all frames, what can you say?"[10]

Hacking is more cautious than Goodman, and although he identifies himself as a social constructionist, he regards as untenable the strong version of social constructionism associated not only with Goodman but also with ethnomethodologists and other sociologists such as

Barry Barnes and other members of the "Strong Programme in the Sociology of Knowledge" at Edinburgh.[11] Hacking argues that the strong version entails an infinite regress regarding the status of the constructionism thesis itself.[12] Fortunately, we need not address that contested issue here.[13] For the purposes of this essay, it is enough to bracket the strong constructionist claim, since its specific implications are not relevant to the present discussion of human rights. In what follows, we work within the weak constructionist view, namely that the above-mentioned framing perspectives or mental models enable us to interactively construe the data of our shared experiences, and that it is the construed data that we call "facts." What we often call "reality" or "the world" is collectively, or better, socially construed in certain ways such that one cannot get at the source of the data except through these construals.

Hacking adds two important corollaries to the general idea of social construction. The first is that the construction process is inherently historical. We are born into and depend on a world that is historically situated, is linguistically, socially, and culturally defined, and is usually if not always in some process of evolution or change. Embedded in these processes are historical, political, economic, and social narratives that as individuals we have neither created nor consciously chosen. Hacking's point, with which we fully agree, is that these narratives define our early mental models and roles as children, as women or men, as tribal members, as worshippers, as citizens, and so on.[14] These narratives as well as the language in which they are embedded constitute a large part of the background against which individual experiences are understood. They provide the initial conditions for the conceptual schemas that frame all our experiences, and they often direct, influence, or constrain the range of mental models that we learn and adapt. The process itself is dynamic: background narratives are revisable mental models that are neither static nor incommensurable with each other. For these reasons, none of us is identified merely with our socially connected selves or completely determined by our background historical social narratives. "We are at once by-products of, characters in, and authors of, our own stories."[15]

Hacking's second point is more complicated as well as especially relevant to the discourse about human rights. Briefly put, it is that social construction takes place within a historical network or matrix from which ideas are generated. As social beings, each of us is constantly interacting with others, thus affecting and being affected by one another's mental models. Those models in turn are also historically and culturally situated and have been constructed within situational contexts. Out of such interactions, philosophers and social scientists take more or less sharply defined theoretical positions on such topics as the scientific method, the validity of historical models, the social constructions of race, gender, ethnic origin, and sexual orientation, and the meanings of terms such as child abuse, serial killers, and homelessness, but not—except occasionally[16]—human rights. He illustrates his point with the relatively recent socio-legal classification of "the woman refugee":

> The matrix in which the idea of the woman refugee is formed [i.e., the formal classification] is a complex of institutions, advocates, newspaper articles, lawyers, court decisions, immigration proceedings [not] to mention the material infrastructure, barriers, passports, uniforms, counters at airports, detention centers, courthouses, holiday camps for refugee children.[17]

Although mental models are perspectival and hence always incomplete, we are able to improve our constructions of reality by engaging in what Amartya Sen has called "transpositional" assessments. That is, we can step back from a particular conclusion or point of view and take a relatively disinterested "spectator" perspective.[18] Of course, that perspective-taking activity is itself socially constructed from some other perspective or set of perspectives, which in turn implies that such assessments are themselves socially constructed views, such that the higher-order assessments can take into account a wider variety of points of view. This stage-structural model of perspective formation is full of interesting epistemological possibilities that we can only mention here. For instance, studying sets of perspectives can reveal important details about how mental models or narratives work in the course of shaping narratives about our own experiences. Revisions of the schema in question could then produce other mental models that more comprehensively explain a given range of phenomena, processes, or conceptual schemas—including the very important schema called "human rights."

The Social Matrix of Human Rights Theory

It would be a mistake to assume from the socially constructed character of human rights that its extensive and complex philosophical literature does not have its own intellectual integrity, or that technical issues such as the difference between the will and interest accounts of human rights are unimportant. However, it does follow that if we think of rights talk in general as an exchange of socially constructed ideas, then the fact that human rights philosophers do not seem to be able to reach consensus on a theory of human rights should be neither surprising nor distressing. We can identify general simi-

larities among competing rights theories, but the theories themselves are nearly always developed from signif-
icantly different points of view. For instance, in a not
altogether hypothetical example of the will-versus-
interests debate mentioned above, a will or agency theorist would hold that human beings have intrinsic value
just because they are humans or, as Griffin puts it,
because they are normative agents who can make fundamental choices.[19] This means not only that human
beings have value in themselves but also that certain
rights of these beings— namely rights concerning the
freedom to make fundamental choices—precede or, as
Ronald Dworkin puts it, "trump" all other rights.[20] In
contrast, an interest theorist influenced by Shue would
contend that without the basic goods needed to survive
as well as some minimum level of security, it would
make no sense to insist on other rights such as the right
to choose other freedoms, even including (at least for
Griffin) the freedom to choose not to live. From this perspective, the rights to survival and minimum security
are basic and universal because survival and security
are necessary conditions for realizing any other rights.
These include rights that a will theorist—especially an
agency-oriented one like Griffin—would count as basic
human rights, since interests in survival and security are
not unique to human beings or (still more restrictively)
to fully competent persons. The interest theorist would
retort that without the means to survive and be minimally safe from harm, other right claims make no
sense—at which point the ball goes back into the other
court.

Admittedly, this thumbnail sketch grossly simplifies
the ongoing debate between proponents of interest-
based and will or agency-based theories of human
rights. However, it illustrates the larger point that those
who hold well-formed opposing theories such as the

ones just mentioned seldom actually resolve their differences even when they recognize considerable value in each other's perspectives. While most will theorists admit the importance of basic goods such as the rights to life, survival, and security, and while most interest theorists acknowledge the importance for human beings of liberty of choice, part of what remains at issue is the prioritization of these rights claims or, more simply, the question: Which rights trump the others and when? In short, when all is said and done, the two sets of theorists are still at an impasse. To use the language of divorce courts, they have irreconcilable differences.

A different, more productive, approach would be to recognize that these seemingly irreconcilable differences are rooted in the different mind sets and social agendas through which philosophers as well as non-philosophers socially construct and give meaning to their own experiences. This approach opens onto a broad avenue where they can engage in an ongoing conversation not about ranking various rights claims but rather about the critical importance of rights talk itself, which is to say talk that not only engages and recognizes differences but also achieves a fair degree of consensus on the more basic idea that human beings do indeed have rights, and that these rights, however prioritized, are charged with moral urgency.

Some might object that this approach leads to hopelessly relativist positions, but we argue otherwise, in spite of the well-known fact that philosophers, politicians, jurists, and social activists regularly disagree on which rights are the most basic, whether there are positive rights as well as negative ones, and whether and how agency-based and interest-based views have each made important contributions to the discussion. Since we understand rights talk as a series of, for the most part, separable proposals that are based on different uses of the term "human rights," we see no reason to demand that human rights theorists agree on the definitions or implications of every right, or on their prioritizations, or on whether a unified theory of rights is even plausible. In the absence of a full consensus, one could adopt the approach that Michael Walzer has taken toward debates about the concept of justice. He observes that despite thousands of pages of discussion, we still disagree on the nature, content, and scope of what is just or fair. However, Walzer goes on to say, we have a great deal of consensus on what counts as *injustice.* In the same vein, we could reasonably hope for a general, albeit incomplete, consensus on specific human rights issues, such as whether there are certain minimal negative rights (e.g., the right not to be tortured, maimed, raped, coerced, or deliberately murdered) that virtually all theorists and persons in the street would agree are worth instituting or preserving even as they continue to disagree on the existence, definition, and prioritization of more robust positive rights, such as the freedom to integrate or to have a certain minimal standard of living. Such a consensus would also allow additions to the roster of human rights, such as the relatively recent addition of the right to privacy (which comes out of late 19th century jurisprudence and varies across communities and cultures) or the right to a livable environment (even though dialogue over environmental issues is still very much in its early stages).[21]

A social construction approach recognizes that that any viable theory of human rights is situated within a historical, social, and cultural context. For instance, it is important to recognize the historical fact that the *United Nations Universal Declaration of Human Rights* was published in the wake of the Second World War and the great horror of the Holocaust. The abrogation of respect for human life and dignity that the Holocaust repre-

sented was a powerful catalyst for writing this document, although we know that Locke and Jefferson anticipated some of its ideas in their own writings. Moreover,
the Universal Declaration was created in a complex process that included many starts and stops as well as several written versions. Initiated by United States President Harry S. Truman, a commission was formed in
1947 consisting of delegates from a wide number of
global regions (although none were from the African
continent). One of the commission's more contentious
issues was the prioritization of rights. France was con-
vinced that the right to conscience was absolutely essential. The Philippines argued for a document that balanced political and economic rights. The United States
stressed basic individual rights, but Yugoslavia argued
for a document that balanced individual and collective
interests. The Soviet Union, while supporting a right to
work as one of the articles in the *Declaration,* argued
that it must also include a duty to the community. There
were also debates about the very nature of rights. The
Italian philosopher and statesman Benedetto Croce
claimed that the point of human rights was to protect
basic needs, whereas others contended that basic rights
should guarantee health and a right to meaningful work.
Still others, such as the neo-Thomist philosopher
Jacques Maritain, tried to construct a master list of
rights from all the major philosophical and religious
points of view. There was also a great debate as to
whether Article 1 of the Declaration should read "All
human beings ... are endowed by nature with reason and
conscience." (The "by nature" phrase was eventually
stricken from the final document.) There was little controversy over the right to life, but the Soviets wanted to
add an amendment abolishing capital punishment. The
right to enter marriage only with equal consent of both
parties was hotly debated, but finally passed. Even the

term "Universal" in the title was a result of a number of conversations, replacing the initial term "international." Indeed, every paragraph in this document of thirty articles was debated and contested.[22]

The *Declaration* that resulted was an imperfect but forceful socially constructed aspirational document that included political rights to life, human dignity, and freedom; economic rights including rights to work, equal pay, and even a holiday with pay; and duties to one's community. As one commentator has noted, "Although the idea of human rights is riddled with notions of natural law, humanitarian intervention, and various hidden agenda[s], ... individuals have banded together to produce documents such as the United Nations Universal Declaration of Human Rights."[23] While every rights theorist can debate some parts of the list, the document stands as a socially constructed testimony of good will, even though it is surely subject to further revisions. For instance, it does not adequately take into account the standing of organizations and communities as possible rights bearers. In sum, this is a socially constructed, largely aspirational document created by a culturally and philosophically diverse committee as part of a larger ongoing dialogue in which individuals and states attempt to bring together many diverse perspectives.

Finally, a social construction account of human rights would also allow a version of human rights theory that accommodates those non-liberal societies that Rawls has called "decent peoples," for whom the very notion of rights is problematic.[24] These are for the most part non-Western societies with historical traditions in which communal needs (including the needs of micro-communities such as the family), rather than the needs or rights of individuals, take precedence, and solidarity is prized over individual freedoms. In other words, in much of the non-Western world, collective interests or rights trump individual claims. An interesting and at least partly successful attempt to have things both ways is the African Charter of Human and People's Rights, adopted in 1981 by the Organization of African Unity (OAU), which specifies not only the rights that individuals have vis-à-vis their governments but also the rights that their collectives (the "peoples") have vis-à-vis other nations, especially their former colonial masters. Unfortunately, the meaning of the term "peoples" was not spelled out in that document, which has led some (primarily Western) critics to conclude that its emphasis on collective rights was not a genuine value but only a cynical strategy to promote the interests of the local ruling groups or classes.[25]

Obviously, this is a disputed issue. Other non-Western societies have worked out promising alternative strategies for achieving the positive values and benefits articulated in the UN Declaration and related documents, such as by adapting classical virtues such as filial piety to the social changes that have come about, at least in part, as a result of the new global economy.[26] In such contexts, the basic idea of human rights is modified but not destroyed. Leaving aside dictatorships and other oppressive societies in which supposedly communitarian maxims are really just propaganda devices for preserving an unjust power structure, there is no principled reason to regard non-Western, communitarian societies as human rights violators. In the absence of evidence to the contrary, we may assume that the citizens of communitarian nations have internalized an "all for one and one for all" ethic and hence are freely submitting to practices and living conditions that might not be accepted in more liberal (and typically Western) societies.

The Ongoing Philosophical Conversation

It should be clear by now that there is a large difference between the social constructionist approach described above and the methodological assumptions of most human rights theorists, especially those philosophers who work in the Anglo-American analytic tradition. Like their philosophical colleagues in metaethics, epistemology, and aesthetics, they usually understand their respective formulations "progressively," which is to say as increasingly accurate accounts of the foundation, definition, and nature of human rights. Philosophers tend to be especially proud of their forensic skills, and relish professional debates in which they can expose one another's ambiguities, confusions, and (best of all!) logically fallacious thinking. Much of the current philosophical literature on human rights proceeds in this manner, even though there are different views of what counts as ample justification for philosophical positions regarding such foundational issues as the nature of human rights.

In this respect James Griffin is an exception. He has explicitly called into question his profession's forensic self-image, first in the introduction to his book *On Human Rights* and later in his response to the contributors to the aforementioned symposium that was devoted to that book, especially to its central thesis that human rights are protections of our "normative agency" rather than of our interests or well-being.[27] Although Griffin does not explicitly identify his approach as social construction, it seems to us that he clearly models that approach. For instance, he opens his book with a very useful distinction between the "systematic" and "piecemeal" approaches to human rights. As he explains, the first and seemingly more rational approach, illustrated by Carl Wellman's *An Approach to Rights*,[28] begins with a general theory (for Wellman it was a theory of value) and then drills down to more circumscribed theories about specific topics such as human rights. The alternative approach, which Griffin himself takes, begins with an expressly historical notion of human rights, which he identifies as the notion that history has bequeathed us. In other words, Griffin believes that the philosophical concept of human rights is best understood as the negotiated response made by a specific intellectual community to its perceived need for a theory that can interrelate and make sense of a wide set of historical "pieces," of which some are new philosophical insights and formulations and others are important worldly events such as the rise and fall of the Roman Empire, feudalism, the Thirty Years War, the invention of the steam engine, and of course the Holocaust.

The current notion of human rights, which is heavily influenced by the diverse phenomena of globalization, is Griffin's own starting point. He justifies his preference for the piecemeal over the systematic approach on several grounds: the systematic approach has not been successful, the very word "right" is too context-specific for any meaningful formal definition, and—for him most important of all—the systematic approach does not seem necessary to achieve the social goals assumed in most of today's human rights discourse.

Griffin goes on to illustrate in several ways the relatively pragmatic character of his conception of the way human rights should be discussed. Three are especially relevant here. The first is his willing admission that his account of human rights was deliberately selective in that certain points were either omitted or deemed not critical to his account of human rights as guarantors of normative agency. The second way is his contrast between what might be called reconstructions and replacements of the concept of rights in general as well as the narrower concept of human rights. Griffin observes that when Kant and Mill commandeered the term "rights" for their own use they were actually "changing the subject," by which he means that they were not proposing new, richer, and more precise definitions of the term "rights," but simply recycling it to designate something altogether different.[29] To put his point more technically as well as more generally, when contemporary human rights philosophers attempt to clarify the meaning of the term "rights," it is often unclear whether they are calling for revisions in the current extension of the term or its current intension.[30] For example, in the above-mentioned debate between interest- and will-theorists of human rights, we must ask whether an author's proposed reformulation of the conceptual link between interests and rights actually advances our understanding of the term "rights" or simply introduces a new subject for discussion.

A second, somewhat more unsettling, example is the challenge made in the same symposium by the jurisprudence scholar John Tasiolas. He asks whether Griffin's agency-based version of the will theory of human rights does not actually brush out the logical correlation between rights and duties which, as we saw above, lies at the center of the usual intension of any conception of rights. As Tasiolas puts it, Griffin "neither draws on, nor supplies, an account of the general nature of moral rights that explains why human rights properly qualify as individual moral rights, as opposed to interests, values, claims, goals, or moral considerations of some other kind."[31] Here he cites the wry comment of James Nickel, another critic of Griffin, that "lest we miss the obvious, human rights are rights."[32] This comment summarizes their shared view that because Griffin does not discuss the duties that others have toward a "normative agent," it is meaningless for him to speak of such an agent as having human rights. (A side note: Griffin's responses to this and other telling criticisms made in the symposium are interesting in themselves, not only because they force him to admit that his own approach still has unsolved problems but also—and more importantly here—because they illustrate the unfinished, construction-in-progress character of the whole discussion of human rights.)

A third illustration of Griffin's pragmatic, constructionist approach is his treatment of the above-mentioned "civil liberties" types of rights, especially the right of free speech. He is uncomfortable with the claim made by some human rights activists that free speech in general and freedom of the press in particular are timeless inalienable rights, but he allows the possibility that even in medieval hamlets people had a (human) right to engage in some forms of what he calls "freedom of expression." He does not spell out the formal features of this right, presumably because it would be anachronistic to do so, but he does insist (as would any confirmed social constructionist) that only in the present era do there seem to be grounds for considering the specific conception of freedom of the press as a legitimate local application of the general concept of human rights.

These illustrations from one highly regarded philosopher's own work show the possibility of a new, more explicit use of social construction theory in the extensive and complex philosophical literature of human rights. Sociologists, political theorists, and anthropologists have already embraced this approach, often going so far as to say that the concept of human rights is not only a historically conditioned construction but also an almost exclusively Western one. We briefly addressed that claim in the previous section, but now add not only that the massive changes gathered under the umbrella label of "globalization" provide the social and cultural environment for new philosophical conversations across regional lines but also that these changes may reveal in non-Western societies something analogous to the Western concept of human rights. In other words, although there is no formal or "metatheoretical" reason to think that Western human rights theory and its non-Western analogues are destined to merge, given their public character and the increasing power of the forces of globalization it seems reasonable to expect some sort of mutual influence between these conceptions. For example, such conversations may reveal that non-Western societies do in fact regulate themselves with what might be called "indigenous analogues" to the human rights conceptions currently in play at the United Nations and the so-called Western world,[33] with the important difference that in those analogues the core philosophical concept is not rights in the sense of claims that individuals make on each other or on their governments, but rather virtues such as loyalty, solidarity, or some other communitarian value.

This way of differentiating Western and non-Western societies recapitulates a distinction that many Western philosophers and social theorists have already made within their own cultures, namely the distinction between liberal, rights-oriented models of civic life and communitarian, virtue-oriented models. Over the last two or three decades, Western philosophers such as Alasdair MacIntyre, Michael Walzer, and Charles Taylor have pushed back against the surge of interest in the liberal, rights-oriented social philosophy that was stimulated by Rawls's *Theory of Justice* and his later works. Since then, many American and European intellectuals and pundits have decried the growing individualism and litigiousness of their fellow citizens, as well as the erosion of social capital by patterns of what the sociologist Robert Putnam has called "bowling alone."[34] In the 1990s, the so-called liberal-communitarian debate grew less shrill, and its participants began to identify themselves as liberal communitarians or communitarian liberals.[35] Our own reading of the international scene is that a similar reconciliation is now taking place between Western and non-Western intellectuals regarding the conceptual issues associated with human rights. However, the most important reconciliation will probably come as a by-product of social changes, not (except indirectly) from philosophical dialectics. Philosophical symposia and other academic exercises in cross-cultural forensics are certainly useful and interesting, but it seems safe to say that global economics and international politics will be the primary matrices for any substantive reconstructions of the conceptions of human rights, of non-Western normative schemas, or—even more probably—of any merger between them.

Conclusion

Echoing Winston Churchill's remark that democracy is the worst form of government except for all the others that have been tried, we would summarize the points made in this article by declaring that the social construction model of human rights is the most tenuous philosophical account except for all the rest. Like most philosophers who have been taught to appreciate what Michael Gardiner has called the polysematicity of philosophical terms,[36] we conclude that any social construction approach is imperfect, especially when what is sought is a definitive definition and analysis of human rights. However, we also believe that, all things considered, the social construction approach provides the best available account of the continuing controversies over rights, as well as the best key for understanding and respecting those communities that do not subscribe to the UN formulations of human rights and yet manage to respect and protect their members. This approach also has room for those cultures that prioritize the community by letting communal values trump individual rights, particularly in moments of crisis. By proceeding from the premise that the abstract philosophical model of human rights is not an eternal truth but rather a historical phenomenon and the result of extended (and still ongoing) conversations, the social construction approach clarifies what is at stake in the different perspectives that are taken in these conversations. This approach encourages such dialogues despite the improbability of full consensus, and yet without denying that there could be a set of general normative principles that all peoples would find acceptable.

Notes

1. For us, the word "concept" is an umbrella term covering a plurality of relatively specific conceptions, just as H. L. A. Hart's "concept of law" and John Rawls's "concept of justice" cover a plurality of related but importantly different uses of those two terms. See Hart, *The Concept of Law* (Oxford: Oxford University Press, 1961); Rawls, *A Theory of Justice* (Cambridge: Harvard University Press, 1971), and Robert Nozick, *Anarchy, State, and Utopia* (New York: Basic Books, 1974).
2. For example, see J. M. Finnis, *Natural Law and Natural Rights* (Oxford: Oxford University Press, 1980), and R. P. George and C. Tollefsen, *Embryo: A Defense of Human Life* (New York: Doubleday, 2008).
3. James Griffin, *On Human Rights* (Oxford: Oxford University Press, 2008).
4. Ian Hacking rings the changes on the terms "construction," "constructivism," and "constructionalism," but concludes that "the themes and attitudes that char-

acterize these 'isms' are not so different." Hacking, *The Social Construction of What?* (Cambridge: Harvard University Press, 1999), 48-44.

5. See Peter Senge, *The Fifth Discipline* (New York: Doubleday, 1990; 2006), and Patricia H. Werhane, *Moral Imagination and Management Decision-Making* (New York: Oxford University Press, 1999).

6. As Carol Gould has put it, social epistemology studies "the ways in which processes of knowledge creation and human modes of cognition can be said to structure or constitute what is known." See Gould, *Constructivism and Practice: Toward a Historical Epistemology* (Lanham, MD: Rowman and Littlefeld, 2003), ix.

7. Werhane, *Moral Imagination,* 53.

8. See Senge, *The Fifth Discipline;* Werhane, *Moral Imagination;* Hacking, *Social Construction;* and Michael Gorman, *Simulating Science* (Bloomington, IN: Indiana University Press, 1992).

9. Hacking, *Social Construction,* 24 (emphasis added).

10. Nelson Goodman, *Ways of Worldmaking* (Indianapolis, IN: Hackett Publishing, 1978), 2-3.

11. See Barry Barnes, *The Elements of Social Theory* (London: UCL Press, 1995).

12. Hacking, *Social Construction,* 37, 65. See also Finn Collin, *Theory and Understanding: A Critique of Interpretive Social Science* (London: Basil Blackwell, 1985).

13. For a relatively "strong" version of social constructionism see Thomas Wren, *Conceptions of Culture* (Lanham, MD: Rowman and Littlefield, 2012), 161-63. For a relatively "weak" version, see Werhane, *Moral Imagination,* 53, and Patricia Werhane, Taraz Radin, and Norman Bowie, *Employment and Employee Rights* (Boston: Basil Blackwell, 2003), especially Chapter 1.

14. Hacking, *Social Construction.* See also Alasdair MacIntyre, *After Virtue* (Notre Dame: Notre Dame University Press, 1981), 199-201.

15. Patricia Werhane, Laura Hartman, Crina Archer, Elain Englehardt, and Michael Pritchard, *Obstacles to Ethical Decision-Making* (Cambridge: Cambridge University Press, 2013), 21.

16. One exception to this generalization is Benjamin Gregg, *Human Rights as Social Construction* (New York: Cambridge University Press, 2012), who takes vigorous exception to the notion of a metaphysical base for any theory, including theories of rights and human rights.

17. Hacking, *Social Construction,* 10.

18. Amartya Sen, "Positional Objectivity," *Philosophy and Public Affairs* 22, no. 2 (1993): 126-45.

19. In what follows we take Griffin's normative agency approach as the most adequate representative of will theory.

20. Ronald Dworkin, *Taking Rights Seriously* (Cambridge: Harvard University Press, 1978).

21. Michael Walzer, *Thick and Thin* (Notre Dame: Notre Dame University Press, 1994).

22. See Joseph Wronka, *Human Rights and Social Policy in the 21st Century* (Lanham, MD: University Press of America, 1992), 85-112; and Johannes Morsink, *The Universal Declaration of Human Rights: Origins, Drafting, and Intent* (Philadelphia: University of Pennsylvania Press, 1999).

23. Wronka, *Human Rights,* 123.

24. John Rawls, *The Law of Peoples* (Cambridge: Harvard University Press, 1999).

25. Rhoda Howard-Hassmann, *Human Rights in Commonwealth Africa* (Totowa, NJ: Rowman and Littlefield, 1986), 2-15.

26. The literature on the so-called Asian Values Debate is quite sophisticated, especially its explication of the relationship between human rights and socio-cultural concepts like "the Asian Identity." On this topic and

other East-West discussions of human rights, see Thomas Wren, "Principles and Moral Argumentation," *Journal of Chinese Philosophy* 16 (1989): 309-15; Lynda Bell, Andrew Nathan, and Ilan Peleg, eds., *Negotiating Culture and Human Rights* (New York: Columbia University Press, 2001); and Peter Van Ness, ed., *Debating Human Rights: Critical Essays from the United States and Asia* (London: Routledge, 1999).

27. The symposium took place in *Ethics: An International Journal of Social, Political, and Legal Philosophy* 120, no. 4 (2010): 679-760. Its participants were all prominent philosophers who have their own strongly held views of human rights, namely John Tasiolas, Allen Buchanan, Rainer Forst, and of course James Griffin.

28. Griffin cites Carl Wellman's *An Approach to Rights* (Dordrecht: Kluwer, 1997) several times in Chapters 4 and 12 of *On Human Rights;* see also Carl Wellman, *A Theory of Rights* (Lanham, MD: Rowman & Allenheld, 1985).

29. "Neither Kant nor Mill was trying to explore the notion of human rights as it appears in [their] historical tradition. They were just commandeering the term 'human rights' (or 'natural rights' or, in Mill's case, just plain 'rights') to do service in the exposition of their own general moral theory. There is nothing wrong with that so long as we are not misled by it. The extension of their term 'rights' is so substantially different from the extension of the [pre-Kantian] Enlightenment notion that we may well think that Kant and Mill are introducing a different concept, that they are, in effect, changing the subject" (Griffin, *Human Rights,* 1).

30. This bit of philosophical jargon refers to a seemingly simple distinction often used in the literature of analytic philosophy. A term's extension is its range of reference (i.e., the things it points to) and its intension is its sense or meaning (i.e., the ideas that constitute its definition).

Here we pass over the fact that some philosophers think the distinction is not simple at all (see Wren, *Conceptions of Culture,* 6-13).

31. Note that Tasiolas's contribution to the symposium is entitled "Taking Rights Out of Human Rights," *Ethics* 120 (2010): 647-78.

32. James Nickel, *Making Sense of Human Rights* (Oxford: Wiley-Blackwell, 2007), 9.

33. Presumably such conversations would suspend the question of whether the objections that political leaders of those societies sometimes make to human rights declarations are truly representative of the citizens of those societies.

34. Robert Putnam, *Bowling Alone* (New York: Simon and Schuster, 2000).

35. See for example, David Bell, *Communitarianism and Its Critics* (New York: Oxford University Press, 1993); Elizabeth Frazer, *The Problem of Communitarian Politics: Unity and Conflict* (Oxford: Oxford University Press, 1999); and Thomas Wren, "The Liberalism-Communitarian Debate," in Patricia Werhane and Edward Freeman, eds., *The Encyclopedia of Business Ethics* (Oxford: Blackwell's, 2002).

36. Michael Gardiner, *Dialogics of Critique: M. M. Bakhtin and the Theory of Ideology* (New York: Routledge, 1992), 193.

3

Educating for Human Rights Consciousness

*Michelle J. Bellino**

Introduction

Since the peace process following Guatemala's 36-year civil war, the state has witnessed a surge in NGOs and INGOs devoted to rights-based issues, has established National Human Rights Institutions to uphold rights domestically, and has committed itself to human rights education (HRE) in the national curriculum, changes which have contributed to a dramatic increase in human rights awareness across civil society. As part of the transition from an authoritarian state associated with massive human rights violations to a pluralistic democracy

*The author would like to thank Myra Levinson, Klaus Neumann, Felisa Tibbits, and Judith Torney-Purta for encouraging and supporting this work.

respectful of ethnic and cultural diversity and human rights of all peoples, one of the goals impressed upon educators has been to instill a culture of human rights among youth of the postwar generation.

Accordingly, national education reforms in Guatemala's postwar years have centered on supporting civic skills and human rights awareness, while largely silencing historical analysis of the causes and consequences of the armed conflict.[1] Curricular material exploring human rights is systematically disarticulated from discussions of the armed conflict, and makes little mention of ongoing violations taking place in the contemporary "postwar" period. Young people across the country learn about Guatemala's experiences with social and political violence more often through silences, evasions, and contestations than by coherent narratives. These silences penetrate homes, communities, and classrooms, where parents and educators report a number of challenges in teaching the violent past.[2]

Although the formal curriculum presents Guatemala's respect for human rights as a positive outcome of the postwar transition, the study described here demonstrates that young people routinely call on instances of human rights in the expression of their absence or violation.[3] Consequently, the ways young citizens interpret human rights, namely in terms of who deserves them, who abuses them, and who suffers for them, as well as whether rights can be effectively advocated by civil society, are intricately related to how youth understand their country's past and present experience with human rights violations. In these ways, historical narratives and human rights consciousness co-construct one another.

HRE has been linked to a number of positive changes in student performance and school culture, and has been recognized as an effective support for youth civic engagement in countries with stable democracies, with added potential in post-conflict contexts.[4] However, in the backdrop of Guatemala's "postwar" violence and instability (two confounding variables in any context), it is unclear whether these curricular reforms (a) are effective at achieving their intended goals of fostering informed and engaged attitudes toward human rights, (b) carry the same human rights potential when disarticulated from coverage of recent conflict, and (c) are interpreted as valuable and valid stances by students and members of civil society.

Often educational policies are authored and implemented without sufficient evaluation of how young learners interpret their experiences through various educational exchanges embedded in broader sociocultural contexts.[5] This contextual interplay is a critical factor in transitional states where new relationships between public and private discourses are negotiated.[6] As stories of suffering are publicly acknowledged, private experiences are narrated according to new discursive boundaries, available "templates," and "cultural repertoires," all of which frame and constrain shared experiences.[7]

This study aimed to shed light on how Guatemalan adolescents construct human rights consciousness, drawing on the language and principles of human rights to generate their own narratives about past and present violence. Likewise, young people draw on their interpretations of Guatemala's experience with violence as they generate new, and often subversive, human rights discourses. In the process, postwar generation youth construct their sense of justice and accountability, framed by the possibilities of human rights ideals, and constrained by the limitations of the "postwar" context. Through ethnographic portraits of formal and informal educational interactions and interviews with youth situated in urban and rural communities, I explore how young people draw on the multiple histories and silences that they have been presented with and how they appropriate human rights concepts in ways that facilitate narratives of violation, based on their lived experience and impressions of the nation's history of violence. Young peoples' attitudes toward human rights pivot along accounts of past and present injustice, exhibiting three contrasting stances, namely, denial, skepticism, and empowerment.

In what follows, I draw on youth perspectives to develop a typology that encompasses narratives of denial in which adolescents reject the normative claims of the human rights framework, narratives of skepticism in which they question whether human rights can be effectively practiced in the Guatemalan context, and narratives of empowerment in which they embrace justice initiatives for past and present violence through the lens of human rights. I begin by examining the history of armed conflict and its aftermath, extending attention to curricular reforms in the educational sector where human rights principles have received added significance. I then explore those three narrative perspectives through ethnographic data, describing educational spaces where young people develop human rights knowledge and attitudes and showing the way they root these narratives in a particular "take" on Guatemala's protracted experiences with violence, as well as in their impressions of how the nation has reconciled with the recent past. I close by discussing the educational implications of these human rights orientations and the civic stances they enable in a fragile, "postwar" democracy.

The Armed Conflict and Its Aftermath

Since Guatemala's beginnings as a state, policies have been in place to discriminate, assimilate, and eliminate the majority indigenous population.[8] Guatemala's civil war, often referred to as the "armed conflict," spanned more than three decades, from 1960 to 1996.[9] The peace process that followed the conflict required nearly a dozen years for state and guerrilla actors to settle on a set of Peace Accords intended to transition the state into democratic stability. Among the proposed resolutions were several explicit transitional justice mechanisms, such as a truth commission, monetary reparations for victims, and a law that allowed for provisional amnesties. Other mechanisms, such as educational reforms, were cast as guarantees of social rights in what was titled the "Agreement on Identity and Rights of Indigenous Peoples."

Led by the United Nations, the Guatemalan Commission for Historical Clarification (CEH) undertook a rigorous inquiry into the armed conflict, revealing a horrific story of egregious human rights violations committed by the state, as well as an armed resistance movement that in some cases was more feared than supported by the communities it claimed to protect. The CEH account estimated that 200,000 people were "disappeared" and 1,000,000 displaced during the course of the conflict, attributing 93% of the human rights violations to the state military, paramilitary, and police, leaving the guerrilla forces responsible for 3% (with the remaining 4% unknown).[10] Furthermore, the CEH concluded that the conflict constituted genocide targeting Guatemala's indigenous Mayan populations, most of whom were unarmed civilians who were not members of the organized resistance movement. The CEH worked to contextualize this conflict as part of a persistent history of state repression toward civil society resistance, exposing a culture of fear employed by the Guatemalan state as a tactic to dispel popular opposition in the state's violent pursuit of nation-building.[11]

Though one of the CEH's recommendations for reconciliation was a public acknowledgement of the scale of violence and rights violations committed during the armed conflict, the state first reluctantly tolerated the Commission and then openly denounced its findings.[12] Denial of the genocide continues today by state officials, many or most of whom were wartime actors who have retained or regained power in postwar years.[13] Meanwhile, efforts to continue historical investigation, locate and identify disappeared bodies, and hold perpetrators accountable have coincided with an onslaught of "memory wars" aimed at silencing individuals and institutions, while destroying documents and spaces involved in the pursuit of historical memory.[14] In particular, human rights activists have become frequent victims of this politicized iteration of postwar violence.[15]

As Guatemala's so-called "postwar" homicide rate has increased to one of the highest in the contemporary world, the state's lack of accountability for past and present violence is magnified by the symbolic adjustment to the language of human rights.[16] Current President Otto Pérez Molina, who took office in early 2012, is a former military general, the first military officer to hold this position in over twenty years. President Pérez Molina has publicly denied that the armed conflict included genocide. He has also been implicated in war crimes, all of which shows the staggering scale of impunity afflicting the country.[17] Despite the nation's destructive legacy of military repression, the rise of contemporary violence has led to a nostalgia for the authoritarian past, contributing to popular calls for the remilitarization of society and the implementation of zero-tolerance security practices, such as *mano dura* (iron fist) policies that create order and counter crime with violence and intimidation.[18]

For some, Guatemala's contemporary violence is a distinctly postwar phenomenon that has little to do with the history of civil war but rather is the result of an influx of deported gang members, organized crime, and regional drug trafficking that has spilled across Guatemala's borders and overwhelmed a weak democracy, coupled with material factors such as poverty, limited opportunity, and a surplus of weapons. For others, past and present violence are intimately linked: amnesty granted to war criminals resulted in a network of "hidden powers" embedded within the state, contributing to the legalization of impunity and the concomitant institutionalization of repression.[19] Different conceptions of peace, justice, and security in the postwar state depend on how these periods of violence are understood, and particularly the temporal linkages between them: that is, whether today's violence constitutes the "postwar" or the "post-postwar" frames that constrain perceptions of the role and responsibilities of citizens and the democratic state.[20] These poles of historical connection and disconnection are well articulated in public and private discourse, and thus provide young people with cultural narratives to which they can attach their personal experiences and impressions of the failing democracy in which they live.

History and Human Rights in the Secondary School Curriculum

When Guatemala's armed conflict ended, negotiators of peace agreements envisioned a shift toward human rights education (HRE) that would emphasize multiculturalism and a "culture of peace," with particular attention to the rights of women, children, and indigenous communities. The approach draws on elements of peace education as well as multicultural and intercultural education, and situates HRE within a broader citizenship education framework.[21] HRE has emerged as a promising educational intervention to promote peace and stability, transformational social change, and an ethical value system, especially following conflict.[22] The United Nations conceptualizes HRE as education that works toward shaping a universal culture of human rights, to be accomplished through the exchange of knowledge and skills, cultivation of appropriate values, attitudes and behaviors, and an understanding of how and when to take action.[23] HRE implies a legal and normative framework where learning content (the material taught) and context (pedagogy, classroom climate) are aligned with human rights principles.[24]

In order to create an authentic culture of human rights, the framework requires firm footing within the curriculum and concrete connections to learners' everyday experiences.[25] Disciplinary connections with historical accounts offer ideal entry points for learning about the past through the lens of human rights, jointly fostering historical understanding and "critical human rights consciousness."[26] Promoting understanding of law, respect for law, and accountability under the rule of law are critical components of the rights-based approach. There is growing empirical evidence that studying historical cases of injustice and rights violations can reinforce respect for human rights, empowering citizens to prevent violence and to intervene when faced with injustice.[27] A number of researchers have extended the study of these "disjunctures" to the present day, advocating that formal educational exchanges open their conversations about justice and democratic ideals by examining the students' everyday experiences with injustice.[28]

The purpose and practice of educating young citizens about historical injustice is contested in all contexts, even in stable democracies.[29] In the aftermath of armed conflict, there is often heated debate about how to represent periods of violence, and whether extensive inquiry into past injustice is unnecessary if not actually a deterrent in fostering a peaceful future.[30] Silencing conflict is not uncommon, and policymakers are increasingly receptive to alternative strategies for building collective identity through shared value systems such as a commitment to human rights, multiculturalism, and a "culture of peace."[31] Guatemala's emphasis on HRE does not demand curricular acknowledgment of its fractured past. Rather than examine the armed conflict through the framework of human rights, the social studies curriculum has become a discussion of abstract rights principles with little mention of national history after the 1960s, when the conflict began.[32] These reforms rest on the expectation that discussions of rights and diversity, though removed from their turbulent historical contexts of inequality and racism, will bring about intercultural understanding through the promotion of the nation's "best story," even with notable gaps.[33]

A content analysis of national curriculum and popular school texts shows that Guatemalan textbooks disproportionately represent the postwar peace process over the conflict itself.[34] Often saturated with the passive voice, the few passages that mention the armed conflict depict state and guerrilla armies as "two devils" who are equally accountable for an extended period of violence, with no mention of state-sponsored genocide or the institutionalization of repression that contributed to violent clashes throughout the state's history.[35] Given shape through the Peace Accords, the armed conflict serves as a moralizing example of the negative consequences of conflict that escalates into violence. For instance, one textbook asks readers, "How did the conflict begin?" and then reasons that "when people cannot agree, when there is abuse by one of the parties, when injustice exists, conflicts are produced."[36] Textbooks often have a chapter devoted to the evolution of human rights, tracing their origin from the Universal Declaration of Human Rights through the Guatemalan peace process, presenting the Peace Accords as an extension of human rights, uniquely serving the nation's indigenous populations. Across curricular materials, one clear objective is the emphasis on individual civic responsibilities in contributing to the peace and stability of Guatemala's postwar democracy. Students are instructed to respect human rights, abstain from drugs and violence, and promote peaceful solutions to conflicts through dialogue and compromise.

A national curriculum is perhaps the most influential form of institutionalized remembering and forgetting for future generations, while conveying embedded models of civic values and participation. Although Guatemala's postwar generation did not directly experience the armed conflict, it did inherit a legacy of violence and has actively constructed interpretations of what this history means for them as citizens of a "postwar" nation. In this way, educational exchanges become one of the most enduring channels through which all segments of society engage with the process of transitional justice, even as collective goals and challenges shift over time. How, then, do young people make meaning of human rights amid the emergence of new violence and the silencing of massive rights violations?

Methodology and Research Context

This paper is based on fourteen months of ethnographic research in Guatemala, spanning 2010-12, in the departments of Guatemala, Izabal, and Sacatepéquez. I designed the study as a comparative ethnography across four urban and rural sites, with the intention of exploring educational opportunities available to young people to learn about the civil war and the postwar transition. In each community, I spent 6-8 weeks as a participant observer, living with families, attending social studies classes, and participating in community events. I collected data in formal and informal educational spaces, including interactions in classrooms as well as community meetings, organized human rights protests, commemorative events, and family dialogues. Interviews with adolescents constitute the focal point of this research, centering on their attitudes toward human rights in Guatemala. In several cases, participating with young people required travel to the province of Sacatepéquez to join active social movements. Additionally, I conducted semi-structured interviews with young people (ages 16-24) in each community context, allowing for further discussion of their individual meaning-making processes around the violent past and the development of their attitudes toward human rights.

Guatemala's history of violence has been intimately linked to geography, politics, and social identity. Most of the armed conflict took place in rural areas and targeted poor, indigenous populations, whereas much of the contemporary violence is concentrated in urban spaces and has different ethnic dimensions. Although today's violence cuts across social classes, touching even those with the most economic and political power, those living in poverty and working class conditions continue to make up the majority of victims.[37] While geography is a signifier of ethnicity and socioeconomic status, social identity is not neatly inscribed in the Guatemalan landscape, and in some cases it shifts across social spaces.

My ethnographic approach has been guided by grounded theory, in that I have aimed to generate new theory as it emerged from the data, through open and focused coding methods. My analytic process has also been informed by theories of culture and collective memory as constituted by "mediated action."[38] In tracing the "cultural tools" that underlie the narratives that young people construct, ethnic identity and geographic location become significant factors in conveying one's proximity to violence, mediating one's claim to the culture of human rights.[39] Cultural tools offer what James Wertsch has called "'constraints' as well as 'affordances,'" in that they make available particular subject positions and stances toward human rights.[40] In turn, the international discourse of human rights "sets the terms within which we can experience our world and also how we can adapt to the potential for our tools to change our world."[41]

The following typology of interpretations sets the stage for analytic claims about the types of relationships that youths construct between their understanding of past violence, contemporary instability, and the various conceptions of human rights. For this reason, I explore the three types of narratives that emerged in the data through interactions with relatively few participants, though these instances illuminate broader patterns. In each case, I highlight a particular educational interaction both to demonstrate that young people construct their understanding of human rights from the interplay between formal and informal learning experiences and to illustrate the way in which particular attitudes and beliefs are given value and affirmation, questioned, contested, and reproduced through these exchanges. However, it is important to note that this typology is not intended to classify or predict how certain categories of youth respond to human rights narratives, but rather to explore the complexity with which all young people construct their human rights consciousness.

Human Rights Consciousness Constructed Through Historical Consciousness

Adolescents vary in their constructions of the relationship that human rights have to their lives, giving shape to three distinct orientations that ground their interpretations of past and present conflicts. In this sense, historical consciousness is a mediating factor in the construction of adolescents' human rights beliefs and their attitudes of denial, skepticism, and empowerment.

Narratives of Denial

Many young Guatemalans maintain strong beliefs that "human rights only protect criminals," faulting the framework for obstructing the state's capacity to administer the death penalty. This narrative carries a visceral denial of human rights even as abstract principles, noting epistemological concerns with what seem to be the artificial guarantee of universal, inalienable, and indivisible rights. Discourses that critique the framework are particularly salient in urban settings, where delinquency is part of everyday life. They are further politicized through a distinct interpretation of historical injustice, namely that Guatemala needs to address contemporary crime as a means of moving forward, thereby "letting go" of the past. Consider the story Eduardo tells.

At six in the morning, Elios drives through grey skies to drop off his twenty- year-old son Eduardo at the university. Eduardo looks blankly out the window as the radio announcer states that two prominent gang members have been caught and are imprisoned awaiting sentencing, each having killed more than a dozen civilians. As Guatemalan adolescents often tell me, it is "a terrible story, but a typical one for Guatemala." Elios lowers the radio and adjusted the mirror to face the backseat, so that our eyes catch. Nodding his head toward me, as if proving something, he asks, "Did you hear that?" He then expresses his doubt that these men will in fact be sent to prison, or that, if sent, they will actually be kept there. Elios and Eduardo exchange glances, and then go on to make casual bets about how long the criminals will be imprisoned before their release and return to a life of violent crime, for which other Guatemalans will pay the price. I try to interject with some optimism, that perhaps these men will be made public examples, deterring future gang violence.

Elios says with a hint of irritation, "Victims are forced to live like criminals ... in order to be safe from criminals who walk free." Eduardo nods, as this conversation is nothing new for him. Since the violent murder of Eduardo's sister, his father has become didactic about the incapacity of Guatemala's justice system, which the family commonly refers to as the "injustice system." Eduardo continues looking out the window, feeling around his pocket for a pack of cigarettes. Shaking one out on his lap, he turns the discussion toward human rights and the death penalty. "These guys should get the death penalty. They killed so many people. Who knows how many they killed? But you can have someone kill a hundred women and still he doesn't get the death penalty. That's when they say, 'Oooh, he has human rights; we can't kill him; we have to protect his rights.'" Turning to Eduardo, Elios continues, repeating what has become a common refrain in the capital city: "Human rights protect killers, while victims live in fear."

Outside the car, Eduardo lights his cigarette, despite his father's disapproving stare from across the street. Elios has been trying to get Eduardo to quit for months, a habit he turned to after his sister's murder. I have heard their claim that human rights only serve to protect criminals, from adults and young people across the capital. When I ask Elios whether he remembers hearing or reading about critiques of human rights, he says, "I didn't need to read about it. It is a simple, observable fact of life in Guatemala." The prevalence of gang violence in Guatemala, linked to transnational criminal networks, routinely asserts itself even from inside prison walls. According to Eduardo, advocating fair trial rights for all perpetrators on the basis of human rights is an exploitation of these ideals. He explains that criminals violate the rights of others until they are caught, at which point they rest on international human rights law to keep them safe. "When they kill, they lose their human rights. When they take away the rights of others, that's when they should no longer have human rights." According to this logic, violence in Guatemala necessitates a rule of law in which human rights are conditional.

Later, Eduardo and I talk at the dinner table, clearing plates. When I ask whether Guatemala's contemporary violence was a consequence of the armed conflict, Eduardo vehemently denies their connections and actively distinguishes them as different types of violence with distinct ideologies. He is not alone in his argument that the country must "let go" of the past so that it can achieve peace. In this way, Eduardo evokes memory as a wall separating Guatemala's violent past from the ideal of peaceful future:

> The problem is that we are still trapped by the past even though this already happened. It is true there was genocide, but when are we going to leave this behind? It is like we are at war today. It is a war.... So why should we talk about the past? Maybe when we have peace, then we can think about it.

Although Eduardo concedes that genocide occurred during the armed conflict, he then expresses nostalgia for the past, first by distancing himself from the lived experience, then by appropriating the perspective of his parents' generation: "I didn't live it, but everyone says it was better when *militares* (military officers) were in charge. Adults know because they lived it, and that's what they say." This slippage toward nostalgia for an era of authoritarian rule, even if accompanied by mass violence, is not uncommon across new or transitional democracies.[42] There is often comfort in recalling an era of order and security, even if it renders mass violence invisible or incidental.

Eduardo's construction of a nostalgic past is informed not simply by his parents' lived experience, but also by a conflation of historical narratives. Occasionally he invokes the official narrative that attributes the conflict to shared accountability between "two devils": "There was genocide, but the guerrillas did a lot of bad too. They killed a lot of people on both sides. Both sides wanted to eliminate each other." Throughout our discussion, Eduardo wavers between this discourse of equal blame, promoted in the national curriculum, and a more politicized one that is in alignment with his parents' views.

> There was a lot of violence. So the state made a curfew, so that no one was on the street at night. When they made this curfew a law, that was when the guerrilla decided to hide in the woods and hunt them [the military]. The military wanted to keep everyone safe, to keep the country safe, but the guerrilla formed armies. They had their own armies ... because they wanted to change the state to a democracy.... And they [the

guerrilla] tried to kill the military and make them leave the pueblo.

In this construction of the past, the guerrilla was the primary aggressor who provoked the state by organizing an armed threat, while the military was forced into violence in order to defend the nation and its citizens. At one point he insists that, despite the brutality of violence during the armed conflict, "at least then, citizens were safe," implying that civilians who were not participating in the conflict were protected by state military actions.

Later, Eduardo says, "Today we have a democracy, but it's a failed one." Because Eduardo faults the guerrilla for the armed conflict, and because he regards the conflict as the precursor to a democratic state, through flawed causal logic he holds the guerrilla resistance movement responsible for Guatemala's failure as a contemporary democratic state. For young people like Eduardo who express nostalgia for the secure past, when citizens "were safe," today's democracy has become synonymous with corruption, violence, and impunity; and human rights are part of these postwar problems. Eduardo considers the United Declaration of Human Rights (UDHR) a set of imported values that the negotiators of the Peace Accords adopted as a concession to indigenous victims, ones that the global community pressures Guatemala to adopt and that the Guatemalan state misappropriates.

> Those human rights only think about the gangs.... They protect the gangs or protect the indigenous, and they say that we ladinos [non-indigenous people] are the exploiters. Human rights—I mean, human rights—should apply to everyone, but if we want to give the death penal-

ty, human rights says we can't kill him to get rid of someone who killed twenty-five children, for example.... I say *derechos de los delincuente* (rights of the delinquent), because they only protect criminals.... With my sister [who was murdered] they stomped on our rights. We have rights too with what happened. My sister had a right to life, but they don't fight for her. Or us.... The only human rights groups that exist, exist for the past. But we are suffering for human rights.... My father fights for his rights, but they don't deliver [the right to justice].... This gives us an environment of more impunity in Guatemala.... Human rights are preventing us from moving out of the present violence.... The UDHR doesn't do anything.

The discussion of human rights evokes deep resentment for Eduardo, and he employs three distinct discourses to account for his estrangement. Initially, Eduardo responds as a victim of contemporary violence whose rights have been violated, but whose violation has been overlooked in the justice-seeking process. His father's pursuit of justice falls on deaf ears in a society where Eduardo's sister is just another victim among many. Eduardo also self-identifies as a member of a socio-ethnic group that is threatened by the implied link between *ladino* and perpetrator, given the history of indigenous exploitation. This frame, which Eduardo perceives as widely shared, makes it difficult to recognize that ladino citizens can also suffer violence and abuse. Finally, Eduardo responds as a citizen of a transitioning democracy concerned that human rights not only hold Guatemala back from ending a violent present but are also responsible for high impunity rates.

In taking up these discourses, his perspective draws on public narratives between which the state's judicial resources have been divided, addressing violence in the past and violence in the present, echoing earlier claims that Guatemala needs to "let go" of the past in order to sufficiently remedy present struggles. Eduardo further validates this past-present divide with a claim that human rights organizations essentially do not "belong" to him—he does not have a right to claim them, as they have been too politically linked to the armed conflict, and therefore are geared toward indigenous rights and justice for past crimes. The three subject positions that Eduardo negotiates merge, rendering him powerless to claim the rights he has been promised.

Narratives of Skepticism

While some young people denounce human rights principles, others express skepticism toward Guatemala's culturally specific social and structural challenges that stand between rights as idealized and rights as actualized. Youth who take up narratives of skepticism implicitly trust the human rights framework but remain cognizant of its unfulfilled promises in their lives, concluding that human rights cannot be effective in Guatemala. This perspective is connected to feelings of shame about the current state of the country, at times linking the armed conflict to the contemporary violence through a lack of reconciliation and an incomplete or "aborted" transitional justice process.[43] Often this fatalism lays claim to a "culture of violence" as an entrenched obstacle that impedes the application of human rights, invoking a radicalized point of view on Guatemala's violent "exceptionalism."

I sit at a desk behind a row of students in Señora Marta's 11th grade social studies class as they finish a unit on human rights. Nearly all students in the windowless room are indigenous, reflecting the composition of both the school and the rural indigenous community in which it is situated. Some girls wear indigenous *traje* (traditional Mayan costume) underneath the school's uniform, a navy sweater with a woven emblem.

Before class, Señora Marta confides that she has mixed feelings about emphasizing human rights to the students in her classes because it feels misleading. "I have to teach about peace and human rights, but unfortunately this is not how the country really is." Although she is conflicted about teaching ideals that are not fully realized, she is confident that her students know the difference between what they learn in school and what they live in everyday experiences. "They don't need me to tell them that peace is not our reality. They know it themselves."

As the buzzer between classes sounds, students diligently rise from their seats and greet us in unison, "Buenos días, Señora Marta," then gesturing toward me, "Buenos días, Señorita Michelle." Señora Marta and I respond in turn, "Buenos días," and the students tuck themselves into their desks. With no prompting, they open their textbooks to the end of the chapter, which was assigned as homework. Though the class has not discussed the armed conflict, the chapter they read closes with several pages outlining the main points of the Peace Accords. Señora Marta begins with a review, "What did the Peace Accords do?" She writes on the board in large letters, "Acuerdos de Paz" (Peace Accords). A few students squirm in their seats, their fingers on the corners of the pages. The teacher begins calling on students by name, and slowly a few hands rise on their own. One student says, "They made men and women equal." Señora Marta nods. Another student adds, "Because of the Peace Accords, we children go to school." Señora Marta's eyes widen in affirmation. When a student says, "The Peace Accords gave human rights to us, the indigenous," Señora Marta folds her hands and smiles, as if that was the answer she was waiting for.

She gestures toward the board and rephrases the student's words, "The Peace Accords gave rights to the indigenous people. What kind of rights?" A list of responses comes forward: the right for indigenous children to attend school, the right to wear the indigenous *traje* instead of uniforms, the right to speak indigenous languages. Student responses typically give voice to the social and cultural rights specific to indigenous communities and populations, many of them rights visible in their current experience (e.g., the right to attend school wearing the *traje*). Though one student mentions that indigenous people now have the right to participate in government, it is notable that political and economic rights, as well as civil liberties, are absent from the discussion. Shifting her tone, Señora Marta asks, "Have the promises of the Peace Accords been realized?" Students nearly respond in unison, and without hesitation, "No." Satisfied with the consensus, and despite the abrupt transition from explicit support for rights to their implicit absence, Señora Marta then moves on to the next chapter on why democratic governments are superior to authoritarian governments.

This interaction demonstrates that even if HRE is inscribed in educational policy, there is no guarantee that this curriculum will be implemented in classrooms, nor does it describe the range of pedagogical approaches that it might yield. Comparative ethnographic cases demonstrate that teachers play significant interpretive roles as mediators of this curriculum, serving as "gatekeepers" of human rights language and principles.[44] Educators' personal histories and experiences interact with the content and context of teaching and learning opportunities they shape in schools, particularly around issues of historical justice.[45] Señora Marta admits the limitations she feels in being inauthentic with her students and promising them "opportunities ... that do not exist for them." Though her lesson might be interpreted as self-defeatist, she views this (largely implicit) critique that she shares with her students as a small act of defiance, a preparation for "the real world." Her own distrust of the human rights framework in Guatemala is apparent, and students share her skepticism.

At lunchtime I sit outside with a group of students on the school steps overlooking the entrance to the pueblo. When I ask them what they meant in class by the unfulfilled promises of the Peace Accords, they share extensive critiques, not only of human rights but also the peace process itself, which failed to fundamentally transform their society. Sixteen-year-old Ixk'at explains:

> I think the armed conflict never ended. On the contrary, violence in Guatemala increases every day.... Some people say this is distinct, this is gang violence today, this is delinquency, but I think it is because the Peace Accords were just a piece of paper. If we really made peace, we would not have so much violence.... It's something we cannot change so easily, to just say we are at peace, when we have been in conflict for so long. Human rights cannot change the culture of violence so easily, not without changing the way Guatemalans think.... Everyone knows that in Guatemala we don't have human rights, we have a culture of violence.

Paco, also sixteen, shares this view. "We are a violent people and a violent country. We have always been a violent country. Human rights will not change that.... That is why the peace process did not work." These young people construct an argument of cultural relativism through the assertion of a "culture of violence" that is incompatible with the fulfillment of human rights. Emphasizing the radical "exceptionalism" of Guatemala's predisposition for violence, these students are skeptical that human rights awareness can transform such embedded attitudes. As Paco puts it, "Violence is who we are ... violence is in our blood." Though he does not see himself, his family, or his close network of school friends as violent, his words convey that "others" make conflict in Guatemala inevitable. Ixk'at continues,

> We are not all equal in Guatemala.... Well, we are, but people don't have respect for equality. People kill for money, or for power, because they don't see people as people, as human, they see them as ... inferior.... That is why human rights cannot be realized here.

These students do not claim to have violent pasts or presents, but to be a "violent people" living in a "violent country," where one's very humanity is called into question by the violent act. The lack of adequate social and political transformation following the war affirms for many young people that the conditions in Guatemala impede the application of human rights. Drawing on discourses of cultural predisposition, they create a concept of exceptionalism, wherein Guatemala becomes the exception to the rule. Human rights may work elsewhere but they are ultimately ineffective in Guatemala, where there are exceptional people and exceptional circumstances. However, because violence permeates everyday experiences, the fault supposedly lies within the hearts and minds of individual Guatemalans who have violent dispositions, who are lured by money to do harm, who do not respect fellow citizens as equal, and who corrupt systems of power. Though the discourse of cultural predisposition renders these young people essentially powerless to change their society, it simultaneously enables them to distance and distinguish themselves from violent actors, whom they can hold accountable for Guatemala's violent exceptionalism.

For many Guatemalan youth, human rights discourse is deeply rooted in the postwar transition and cannot be unhinged from the unfulfilled promises of the Peace Accords. The wide gap between articulated human rights principles and the way they are upheld in practice serves as a reminder of Guatemala's weak and inconsistent application of the rights of its citizens. This gap legitimizes their skepticism toward the human rights framework.

Narratives of Empowerment

Unlike those who mistrust human rights as ethical principles or as legal and social norms, some adolescents draw on human rights as an empowering frame. Drawing on discourses promoted by domestic human rights movements, youths who employ this perspective shape their understanding of human rights around linked narratives of historical injustice and popular resistance. Present-day rights movements themselves draw from the historical narrative constructed by the truth commission in their reports in order to portray their struggle as ongoing.[46] In this interpretation, the link between past and present violence reflects the continuous opposition between the state and civil society, a conflict between those who seek reform in pursuit of equality and those who enact repression in the service of neoliberal nation-building.[47] Young people who construct narratives of human rights empowerment recognize the potential inherent in claiming one's rights and express their willingness to take on the civic responsibilities to hold duty bearers accountable.

In June 2010, thousands of Guatemalans gathered in demonstration against a group of foreign-owned resource extraction companies in the Maya Highlands. The United Nations Special Rapporteur of Indigenous Peoples sat on a stage decorated with pine needles and flowers to hear the people's complaints. In the crowd, the variety of native dress indicated the presence of many indigenous communities, as well as travelers from Honduras and El Salvador who protested in solidarity with them. Testimony after testimony voiced individual and collective violations of land rights, water rights, cultural rights, sexual rights, rights to organize, and the right to life. The field surrounding the stage was filled with people so that no stretch of grass was visible, with many wearing or holding flowers as a symbol of resistance to corporate practices that diverted the village water supply, consequently damaging crops. A nearby school contained several small balconies, where young women stood shoulder to shoulder to listen, their hands wrapped around the thin metal railing. Though they smiled at one another between speakers and while passing around candy, they were expressionless as they listened to the litany of human rights abuses.

Speakers repeatedly drew historical connections between abuses of human rights that took place during the armed conflict and the abuses that continue to exploit and repress indigenous communities today. One man spoke of the long and ongoing history of oppression directed at indigenous populations, declaring, "We suffered colonization.... We suffered genocide in the '80s.... We continue to suffer." Young people carried hand-painted protest signs, many decorated with photographs and names of deceased relatives. Their signs explicitly evoked "the '80s" to conjure memories of the genocidal years, and others drew on the language of human rights, such as the boy and girl who took turns carrying a pink sheet of paper that read, "The biggest crime our parents committed was defending their rights and our future."

Next to me, a small boy hid behind his mother's hip, too young to understand. A sleeping baby rested on the mother's back, held in place with a purple sash. When the demonstration ended, I asked Linda, who was barely 20, about her bringing children to the protest. Although she had pragmatic reasons for bringing them, she also believes that their presence is an early form of human rights education. As she explained,

> The Peace Accords gave us human rights, and this is how to learn about them, when we organize because they are being violated.... We indigenous, we need to know our rights to protect ourselves. So we can say, "This violates the Peace Accords. You need to ask the village if we consent to this mine being here. This violates indigenous rights, because we have the right to say: This is our land and you are taking advantage of us. We have the right to be consulted." One day, my children will need to protect me ... so that what happened to my parents will not happen to me, so that what happens to me will not happen to them [my children].... Unfortunately, this is the history of Guatemala; it is always a risk to struggle for human rights.... That is why we need to continue the struggle.... This is why I am here. I am here for them [my children], to protect the conditions in which they will live.

Linda's comment demonstrates the pressing need for human rights knowledge, particularly rights guaranteed to indigenous communities and codified in the Peace Accords, as a precedent to claiming rights. Given the recurrent history of rights violations, she does not anticipate that the state will ever guarantee the rights of all citizens without struggle; in this sense, it will always fall to marginalized populations to stay vigilant and claim their rights, even at the risk of harm. Linda educates her children so that even though they will inherit better conditions, they will also have the capacity to protect themselves and others. For her, human rights constitute a discourse of power, carrying the possibility for change while also exemplifying the act of change itself.

The young people who joined this protest and others like it often connect historical memory and human rights, at times claiming historical memory itself as a human right. Regina, an indigenous 19-year-old living in a nearby village, integrates her historical consciousness of past and present violence with her human rights consciousness:

The violence today is the same [as the violence of the past]. People don't respect one another.... Respect is the base of all human rights.... Human rights are important to my life, because someday we will need to stand before the PDH [Office of the Human Rights Ombudsman] to defend our rights.... Even when we go there, to a human rights office, we can have our rights violated. Human rights says we treat everyone the same, no matter what they look like or how much money they have. Everyone is the same ... but indigenous rights have been violated repeatedly. We can see this over time from colonialism to today.

Like Linda, Regina anticipates that indigenous rights will continue to be violated, even by state actors. This inevitable pattern of ethnic and class-based discrimination can be interrupted by knowledge of one's rights, but not prevented. Regina goes on to explain that telling her family's story is her right, as well as the best way to achieve "justice for the disappeared." Raul, a youth activist who traveled from the capital to participate in the protest, expresses a similar point of view, further justifying present-day rights struggles with a historical perspective:

> Human rights are the reason we have to fight for justice for the past [for crimes committed during the armed conflict]. What kind of human rights can we have today if we say that you can commit genocide and kill 200,000 people and still be free? And not just free because you have amnesty—you can actually start a profitable business, live a comfortable life abroad, or be elected into state government.... This is why we have a constant struggle ... to move forward memory and justice.

Raul speaks to the declining moral and ethical power of human rights when perpetrators of mass crimes are not held accountable, arguing that justice for past and present violence presupposes a recognition of human rights as well as the rule of law. Others are more pragmatic in their promotion of human rights, linking knowledge to action and action to power. For instance, Karina, fourteen, says, "The armed conflict was the root of all the violence today.... No one is vigilant of the people's rights, but the people can only defend themselves when they are informed." Adolescents who embrace human rights as a frame of empowerment do not regard them as abstract principles but rather as a transactional contract that requires vigilance and civic action, even if this vigilance is itself an additional obligation specific to Guatemala's "postwar" context and those who have inherited the legacies of war.

The indigenous Mayan peoples voicing their suffering at this protest represent a population whose rights have been most egregiously violated in the past and present. Yet these marginalized communities appear to embrace the human rights framework more readily than those whose rights have been historically upheld by the state. What accounts for this seemingly paradoxical embrace of human rights principles when others dismiss them on the assumption that they do not apply to the extreme conditions of "postwar" Guatemala? The discourses underpinning the publicly shared testimonies reveal the usefulness of seeing human rights as a "schematic template."[48] Paradoxically, human rights violations committed by a repressive state toward its citizens become instrumental in discursively situating historical injustice as an ongoing violation. Though multinational corporations are not bound by rights contracts as duty-bearers, activists make clear connections between corporate practices and state complicity. In the process, these actors link violations that might deviate from the traditional frame within rights discourse in order to garner global recognition and support. The idea of human rights has become an organizing concept with international legitimacy as it names and frames the injustices that Mayan communities have experienced over time. These rights discourses are more than merely instrumental means of global recognition; they are also empowering in that knowing one's rights is the key to the call of *Nunca más!* (Never again!) for themselves and for future generations.

Conclusion

Given pervasive violence and impunity, as well as unanswered calls for historical justice, it is not surprising that many Guatemalan adolescents openly question the legitimacy of the human rights framework. Contrary to the intentions of creating a universal culture of human rights, the rights frame is not universally empowering, even in states that are more stable and homogenous than Guatemala. We cannot predict from these data which young people will be more likely to embrace or reject the human rights frame, but we can see that historical interpretations and individual experiences with violence or other sorts of rights violations function as mediating factors in the way young people navigate available rights-based discourses. This typology evokes a new set of questions about how human rights function as a system of belief in the context of a weak state, as well as implications for educational interventions in the aftermath of mass violence.

First, a complex interplay of narratives and beliefs are exchanged through a range of contexts—public and private, intergenerational and transgenerational, as well as explicit and implicit teaching and learning exchanges. Young people construct their historical consciousness, their understandings of human rights, and their relationships with the state through these formal and informal exchanges. In line with existing literature, both schools and daily experiences with the rights contract constitute mediating spaces through which young people construct their understanding of justice, as well as their conceptions of the rights and responsibilities implied in national and universal social compacts.[49] Although young people do not always experience contradictions between in and out of school experiences—and in some cases are exposed to tacit critiques in schools—the gaps between human rights ideals and the way these principles are applied in a "postwar" state are apparent to all young people in their everyday lives. These disjunctures reveal the limits of justice, equality, and rights for all. Although their recognition might take place in formal learning spaces, it is more likely to take place in dialogue between formal and informal settings, such as when Regina learns that her deceased grandfather's body was found in a mass grave, or when a police officer explains to Eduardo's family that there was no investigation for his sister's murder because she looked like a prostitute. These experiences carry enormous weight in young people's construction of human rights consciousness, juxtaposing lived experience with the promised ideals of a universal culture of human rights.[50]

Second, while HRE decoupled from historical injustice may transmit optimism about a potential future that is equitable and just, the evasion of a contentious past undermines agency and may reinforce the conviction that Guatemala's culture of violence has condemned its citizens to a history of violence.[51] Critiques of values-based peace education and the silencing of historical injustice imply that constructing peace around a new set of positive moral principles risks generating personal and cultural attributions for violence, locating social problems within individuals rather than within institutions.[52]

Although human rights education does not prescribe a historical frame or a confrontation of rights abuses, accountability is a key legal and normative element of HRE.[53] Accountability is expected of both state and non-state actors, as both are mutual agents and subjects within the human rights contract. Moreover, as an educational approach, HRE expressly calls for civic action to demand that duty bearers fulfill universal human rights obligations when they are lacking, with civic participation upholding accountability.54 However, this emphasis on personal responsibility and civic participation of individual rights holders may undermine students' capacity to hold an absent state accountable, and instead lead them to blame fellow citizens for replicating violence "in the blood." The focus on individual responsibilities too easily equates the role of individual citizens, state actors, and the structures or institutions that bind them.55 In this sense, there is an important distinction to be made between civic agency and state power.

Whether or not a formal curriculum places human rights into a historical context, young people seem determined to bring both history and the politics of power into the discussion, even when there are fundamental disagreements over who has had access to power and rights over time and space. If utilized as educational partners, HRE and historical inquiry might expand awareness of civic agency, state accountability, and opportunities for participation.

Third, the stances that young people take up reveal that they construct normative claims about the relationship between a state and its citizens based on their understanding of injustice and informed by direct and indirect experiences. Youth variously characterize the state as a protector, a violator, or a democratic partner, as well as powerful, incompetent, abusive, and even, at times, a victim of its own citizens. In each case, young people reassert the critical role of historical consciousness, constructed through a variety of educational exchanges, in shaping their present understandings of state and civic duty to guarantee human rights. While the discourse of human rights "claims the belief"56 of some young Guatemalans, it offers others normative language with which to dismiss the rule of law in a fragile democracy.

Notably, human rights principles depend on the per-ceived legitimacy of a civil contract and a state's capacity to provide basic rights and services to its citizens. Those who reject human rights serve as a reminder that young citizens need to believe in the capacity of their state to uphold the rule of law. This does not mean that human rights discourse is powerless to shape young people's attitudes in the Guatemalan context, or that there is no value to teaching human rights in a society struggling with legacies of injustice and entrenched structures of inequality. As Lynn Davies has argued, despite the chal-lenges of isolating educational effects from other sec-tors, "Analysis is about weighing up opportunity costs of doing and not doing something in the educational realm."[57] With this in mind, we might do better to begin education where young people begin, namely with their lived experience and the gaps through which they filter knowledge of human rights ideals.

Notes

1. See Michelle J. Bellino, "Whose Past, Whose Present? Historical Memory Among the 'Postwar' Generation in Guatemala," in *(Re)building Memory: School Text-books, Identity, and the Pedagogies and Politics of Imagining Community: Vol. 3. Textbooks and Conflict,* ed. James H. Williams (in press); Elizabeth Oglesby, "Educating Citizens in Postwar Guatemala: Historical Memory, Genocide, and the Culture of Peace," *Radical History Review* 97 (2007): 77-98; Elizabeth Oglesby, "Historical Memory and the Limits of Peace Education: Examining Guatemala's Memory of Silence and the Poli-tics of Curriculum Design," in *Teaching the Violent Past: History Education and Reconciliation,* ed. Eliza-

beth Cole, 175-202 (Lanham, MD: Rowman & Little-field, 2007).
2. Bellino "Whose Past, Whose Present?"
3. The Ministry of Education is one example. See *Modulos de Aprendizaje* [Models of Learning], vols. 1-2 (Guatemala City, Guatemala: Ministry of Education, 2003).
4. Tania Bernath, Tracey Holland, and Paul Martin, "How Can Human Rights Education Contribute to International Peace-Building?" *Current Issues in Comparative Education* 2, no. 1 (1999): 14-22; Nancy Flowers, ed., *A Survey of Human Rights Education* (Gütersloh, Germany: Bertelsmann Verlag, 2003).
5. Judith Torney-Purta and Carolyn Barber, "Fostering Young People's Support for Participatory Human Rights through their Developmental Niches," *American Journal of Orthopsychiatry 81,* no. 4 (2011): 473–481.
6. Michael Jackson, *The Politics of Storytelling: Violence, Transgression and Intersubjectivity* (Copenhagen, Denmark: Museum Tusculanum Press, 2006); Eric Stover and Harvey Weinstein, *My Neighbor, My Enemy: Justice and Community in the Aftermath of Mass Atrocity* (Cambridge: Cambridge University Press, 2004).
7. For further information see James V. Wertsch, "Specific Narratives and Schematic Narrative Templates," in *Theorizing Historical Consciousness*, ed. Peter Seixas, 49-62 (Toronto: University of Toronto Press, 2006); Barbara Rogoff, Leslie Moore, Behnosh Najafi, Amy Dexter, Maricela Correa-Chávez, and Jocelyn Solís, "Children's Development of Cultural Repertoires through Participation in Everyday Routines and Practices," in *Handbook of Socialization: Theory and Research,* ed. Joan E. Grusec and Paul D. Hastings, 490-515 (New York: Guilford Press, 2007).
8. Carlos Figueroa Ibarra, *El Recurso del Miedo: Estado y Terror en Guatemala* [The Recourse of Fear: State

and Terror in Guatemala], 2nd ed. (Guatemala: FyG Editores, 2011); Beatriz Manz, "The Continuum of Violence in Post-War Guatemala," *Social Analysis* 52, no. 2 (2008): 151-164.

9. The causes of the civil war are far more complex than can be presented here. See Greg Grandin, *The Blood of Guatemala: A History of Race and Nation* (Durham, NC: Duke University Press, 2000); Beatriz Manz, *Refugees of a Hidden War: The Aftermath of Counterinsurgency in Guatemala* (Albany, NY: State University of New York Press, 1988); Stephen Schlesinger and Stephen Kinzer, *Bitter Fruit: The Story of the American Coup in Guatemala* (Cambridge, MA: David Rockefeller Center for Latin American Studies, 2005).

10. *Comisión para el Esclarecimiento Histórico, Guatemala: Memoria del Silencio* [Guatemala: Memory of Silence] (Guatemala: Comisión para el Esclarecimiento Histórico, 1999).

11. Greg Grandin, "The Instruction of Great Catastrophe: Truth Commissions, National History, and State Formation in Argentina, Chile, and Guatemala," *The American Historical Review* 110, no. 1 (2005): 46-67.

12. Oglesby, "Historical Memory."

13. Susan C. Peacock and Adriana Beltrán, *Hidden Powers in Post-Conflict Guatemala: Illegal Armed Groups and the Forces Behind Them* (Washington, DC: Washington Office on Latin America, 2003); Victoria Sanford, "From Genocide to Feminicide: Impunity and Human Rights in Twenty-First Century Guatemala," *Journal of Human Rights* 7 (2008): 104-122.

14. Michelle J. Bellino, "The Memory War in 'Postwar' Guatemala: Human Rights Activism in the Aftermath of Mass Conflict," in *Human Rights in Times of Transition,* ed. J. Briggs and B. Terminski (in press).

15. *Unidad de Protección a Defensoras y Defensores de Derechos Humanos de Guatemala (UDEFEGUA),* Per-

mitido Denunciar (Guatemala City, Guatemala: UDEFEGUA, 2011).

16. For further statistics see United Nations Office on Drugs and Crime, *Crime and Instability: Case Studies of Transnational Threats* (February 2010).

17. Guatemala Human Rights Commission (GHRC), "Pérez Molina and Baldizón to Compete in Presidential Runoff," *El Quetzal* 10 (2011): 1-3.

18. Peter Benson and Edward F. Fischer, "Neoliberal violence: Social Suffering in Guatemala's Postwar era" in *Mayas in Postwar Guatemala: Harvest of Violence Revisited*, ed. Walter E. Little and Timothy J. Smith, 151-166 (Tuscaloosa: University of Alabama Press, 2009); Anthony W. Pereira and Mark Ungar, "The Persistence of the *Mano Dura:* Authoritarian Legacies and Policing in Brazil and the Southern Cone," in *Authoritarian Legacies and Democracy in Latin America and Southern Europe,* ed. Katherine Hite and Paola Cesarini, 263- 304 (Notre Dame, IN: University of Notre Dame Press, 2004).

19. Peacock and Beltrán, *Hidden Powers;* Sanford, "From Genocide to Feminicide." For further discussion, see Michelle J. Bellino, "Feminicide and Silence in 'Postwar' Guatemala," *Women's Policy Journal of Harvard* 7 (2010): 5-9; Benson and Fischer, "Neoliberal Violence," Deborah T. Levenson, *Adiós Niño: The Gangs of Guatemala City and the Politics of Death* (Durham, NC: Duke University Press, 2013).

20. Michelle J. Bellino "What Kind of History, for What Kind of Citizen?," *Dialogues on Historical Justice and Memory Research and Advocacy Network, Working Paper Series, no. 1* (March 2014).

21. Instituto Interamericano de Derechos Humanos [Inter-American Institute of Human Rights], *Inter-American Report on Human Rights Education, No. 4* (San Jose, Costa Rica: Instituto Interamericano de

Derechos Humanos, 2007); Ministry of Education, Interculturalidad en la Reforma Educativa [Interculturality in educational reform] (Guatemala City, Guatemala: Ministry of Education, 2010).

22. Bernath, Holland, and Martin, "How Can Human Rights Education Contribute?" Lynn Davies, "Building a Civic Culture Post-Conflict," *London Review of Education* 2: 3 (2004): 229-244; Flowers. A Survey of Human Rights Education; Betty A. Reardon, "Human Rights as Education for Peace," in *Human Rights Education for the Twenty-First Century,* ed. George J. Andreopoulos and Richard Pierre Claude, 21-34 (Philadelphia: University of Pennsylvania Press, 1997).

23. UNESCO and UNICEF, *A Human Rights Based Approach to Education for All* (Paris: UNICEF and UNESCO, 2007).

24. Felisa Tibbitts, "Human Rights Education," in *Encyclopedia of Peace Education,* ed. Monisha Bajaj (Charlotte, NC: Information Age, 2008).

25. Felisa Tibbitts and William R. Fernekes, "Human Rights Education" in *Teaching and Studying Social Issues: Major Programs and Approaches,* ed. Samuel Totten and Jon E. Pederson, 87-118 (Charlotte, NC: Information Age, 2011).

26. Garth Meintjes, "Human Rights Education as Empowerment: Reflections on Pedagogy," in *Human Rights Education for the Twenty-First Century,* ed. George J. Andreopoulos and Richard Pierre Claude, 64-79 (Philadelphia: University of Pennsylvania Press, 1997).

27. Robert L. Selman and Dennis Barr, "Can Adolescents Learn to Create Ethical Relationships for Themselves in the Future by Reflecting on Ethical violations Faced by Others in the Past?" in *Interpersonal Understanding in Historical Context,* ed. Matthias Martens,

Ulrike Hartmann, Michael Sauer, and Marcus Hassel-horn, 19-41 (Rotterdam, The Netherlands: Sense, 2009).
28. Monisha Bajaj, *Schooling for Social Change: The Rise and Impact of Human Rights Education in India* (New York: Continuum International Publishing, 2012); Andrea Dyrness, "Contra Viento y Marea (Against Wind and Tide): Building Civic Identity among Children of Emigration in El Salvador," *Anthropology & Education Quarterly* 43, no. 1 (2012): 41-60; Beth C. Rubin, "'There's Still Not Justice': Youth Civic Identity Development amid Distinct School and Community Contexts," *Teachers College Record* 109, no. 2 (2007): 449-481.
29. Gary B. Nash, Charlotte Crabtree, and Ross Dunn, *History on Trial: Culture Wars and the Teaching of the Past* (New York: Vintage Books, 2000).
30. Bellino, "What Kind of History"; Elizabeth A. Cole and Judy Barsalou, "Unite or Divide? The Challenges of Teaching History in Societies Emerging from Violent Conflict," *Special Report* no. 163 (Washington, DC: United States Institute of Peace, 2006), 1-16.
31. See Cole and Barsalou, "Unite or Divide?" Elizabeth A. Cole and Karen Murphy "History Education Reform, Transitional Justice, and Transformation of Identities," *International Center for Transitional Justice* 1, no. 1 (2007): 115-137; Oglesby, "Historical Memory"; Harvey Weinstein, Sarah Warshauer Freedman, and Holly Hughson, "School Voices: Challenges Facing Education Systems after Identity-Based Conflicts," *Education, Citizenship, and Social Justice* 2, no. 1 (2007): 41-71.
32. Oglesby, "Educating Citizens." Educating for Human Rights Consciousness/157
33. Peter Seixas, "Schweigen! die Kinder! or, Does Postmodern History Have a Place in the Schools?" In *Knowing, Teaching, and Learning History: National and International Perspectives,* ed. Peter Stearns, Peter

Seixas, and Sam Wineburg, 19-37 (New York and London: New York University Press, 2000), 20.

34. Bellino, "Whose Past, Whose Present?"

35. Elizabeth Jelin, *State Repression and the Labors of Memory* (Minneapolis: University of Minnesota Press, 2003). Also see Bellino, "Whose Past, Whose Present?" In Oglesby, "Educating Citizens."

36. Ministry of Education, *Modulos de aprendizaje,* 25.

37. Levenson, Adiós Niño; Sanford, "From Genocide to Feminicide."

38. On open and focused coding methods, see K. Charmaz, "Coding in grounded theory practice," in *Constructing Grounded Theory: A Practical Guide through Qualitative Analysis,* 42-71 (Thousand Oaks, CA: Sage, 2006); On mediated action, see Helen Haste and Salie Abrahams, "Morality, Culture and the Dialogic Self: Taking Cultural Pluralism Seriously," *Journal of Moral Education* 37, no. 3 (2008): 377-394; and James V. Wertsch, *Voices of Collective Remembering* (Cambridge: Cambridge University Press, 2002).

39. Wertsch, *Voices of Collective Remembering,* 11.

40. Ibid., 12.

41. Haste and Abrahams, "Morality, Culture and the Dialogic Self," 380.

42. Molly Andrews, *Shaping History: Narratives of Political Change* (Cambridge: Cambridge University Press, 2007).

43. Bellino, "Whose Past, Whose Present?"

44. Stephen J. Thornton, "Teacher as Curricular-Instructional Gatekeeper in Social Studies," in *Handbook of Research in Social Studies Teaching and Learning,* ed. James P. Shaver, 237-248 (New York: Macmillan, 1991).

45. Cole and Murphy, "History Education Reform."

46. *Comisión para el Esclarecimiento Histórico.*

47. See Grandin, "The Instruction of Great Catastrophe"; Manz, "The Continuum of Violence."

48. Wertsch, "Specific Narratives and Schematic Narrative Templates."

49. Constance Flanagan, Tara Stoppa, Amy K. Syvertsen, and Michael Stout, "Schools and Social Trust," in *Handbook of Research on Civic Engagement in Youth,* ed. Lonnie R. Sherrod, Judith Torney-Purta, and Constance A. Flanagan, 307-329 (Hoboken, NJ: John Wiley and Sons, 2010); Torney-Purta and Barber, "Fostering Young People's Support."

50. Michelle J. Bellino, "A History of Violence Argues Against a Culture of Violence," *Revista* 10, no. 1 (2010/2011): 13-16; Oglesby, "Educating Citizens."

51. Bajaj, *Schooling for Social Change.*

52. Oglesby, "Educating Citizens" and "Historical Memory"; Bradely A. U. Levinson, "Forming and Implementing a New Secondary Civic Education Program in Mexico: Toward a Democratic Citizen without Adjectives," in *Reimagining Civic Education: How Diverse Societies Form Democratic Citizens,* ed. E. Doyle Stevick and Bradely A. U. Levinson, 245-270 (Lanham, MD: Rowman and Littlefield, 2007).

53. Nancy Flowers (with Marcia Bernbaum, Kristi Rudelius-Palmer, and Joel Tolman), *The Human Rights Education Handbook: Effective Practices for Learning, Action and Chance* (Minneapolis, MN: University of Minnesota Press, 2000); UNESCO and UNICEF, *A Human Rights Based Approach.*

54. Flowers, *A Survey of Human Rights Education;* UNESCO and UNICEF, *A Human Rights Based Approach.*

55. Monique Eckmann, "The Role of History in Education against Discrimination;" in Human Rights and History: A Challenge for Education, ed. Rainer Huhle, 166-

174 (Berlin: *Stiftung Erinnerung verantwortung Zukunft,* 2010).

56. Stephen E. Toulmin, *The Uses of Argument* (Cambridge: Cambridge University Press, 2003).

57. Lynn Davies, "Can Education Interrupt Fragility? Toward the Resilient Citizen and the Adaptable State;" in *Educating Children in Conflict Zones: Research, Policy, and Practice for Systemic Change,* ed. Karen Mundy and Sarah Dryden-Peterson, 33-48 (New York: Teachers College Press, 2007), 33.

4

Human Rights and the Rest of Us

David T. Ozar

Introduction

Since the 1600s if not before, the language of rights has played an important role in people's claims about how other persons, groups, organizations, and especially governments and nations, ought or ought not to act. Not surprisingly, ever since then philosophers and other political thinkers have studied and theorized about such claims—which I will simply call "rights-claims." However, since the adoption of *The Universal Declaration of Human Rights* by the United Nations General Assembly on December 10, 1948,[1] the theoretical literature on rights, and especially human rights, has grown tremendously.

This literature has focused on three kinds of questions. A lot of it has focused on explaining what makes rights-claims, and especially human-rights-claims, morally or ethically important. Some of it has worked on the closely related question of how to tell whether a particular rights-claim is true. However, in spite of the frequency with which rights-claims are made in our daily lives and in the world at large, a third kind of question remains, namely: What does the claim that someone "has a right" *really mean?* This question has proven even more theoretically complex than the others. If one has a right, does one therefore actually have "something" and, if so, what sort of thing could this "something" be? In what follows I will call this "the meaning-question."

It seems clear that if I truly have a certain right, then someone else—some individual or some group—has an obligation to act or to refrain from acting in some way in regard to me, and this obligation is widely accepted. (Note: Since consciously refraining is itself a type of acting, in what follows the simpler phrase "to act" will often be used for brevity's sake with "to refrain" always implied along with it.) But rights-claims are widely understood to be something more than a simple announcement that another party has a certain obligation. After all, why say this obligation creates "a right" if this does not add anything new to the idea of an obligation, and why say that a right is something that a person or a group "has"? In other words, why indicate (or even just imply) that there is some kind of special relationship between a rights-claim and the claimant? These are some of the puzzles associated with what I have called the "meaning-question" about rights-claims.

This question may seem to be too abstract to be very important. Obviously, people make all kinds of rights-claims without ever needing to ask themselves just what the expression "has a right" really means. However, once we start trying to develop answers to that question, we find that just how we answer it has important implications about when a rights-claim is really true. In other words, how we answer the meaning-question has implications about who really does or does not have certain rights, especially certain human rights, and that is certainly very important.

One of the most widely respected contributions to the study of all three of these questions about rights-claims is an essay published in 1970 by the American philosopher Joel Feinberg entitled, "The Nature and Value of Rights."[2] In that essay, Feinberg proposed an answer to the meaning-question about rights-claims, an answer that has been accepted by many other philosophers and political theorists. However, as Feinberg himself points out, if his explanation is correct, then in spite of their evident moral importance most if not all of the usual human-rights-claims—including those identified in the UN's *Universal Declaration of Human Rights*—must be considered literally meaningless since they lack a crucial component of the meaning of a rights-claim. Note that Feinberg does not deny the moral importance of the things that these "human rights" point to. He only holds that there is a different and perfectly adequate explanation as to why they are so important morally. However, Feinberg thinks that, strictly speaking, we should not call them rights.

He concedes that the language of rights seems to naturally attach to these kinds of moral claims, even though they do not fulfill the meaning-conditions of a rights-claim. He proposes the expression "manifesto rights" as a way of acknowledging that the language of rights seems very appropriate for them. However, Feinberg's argument remains that manifesto rights (i.e., most if not all of the rights commonly called "human rights") are not really rights at all because they fall short of what is required for a meaningful rights-claim.

In what follows, I will argue that the answer that Feinberg has proposed for the meaning-question about rights-claims (and which many other thinkers have since endorsed) is incomplete. I will show that when the meaning-question about rights-claims is answered correctly, many familiar human-rights-claims (including those that Feinberg and others have relegated to the category of manifesto rights on the grounds that they are not meaningful as rights-claims) will be seen to be meaningful rights-claims after all. In correcting our understanding of rights-claims in this way, I will also show why whenever a human-rights-claim is made, it has implications about obligations that the "Rest of Us"—that is, all of us—do indeed have.

Feinberg's Challenge

Feinberg's answer to the meaning-question that he asks in "The Nature and Value of Rights" is not mistaken, only incomplete. To show this and to explain what this point means for human-rights-claims, I will begin where Feinberg does, namely with the very idea of a rights-claim. As he explains, the very definition of a right entails that if a person or group of persons has a right, then there is also some identifiable person or group of persons that has a corresponding duty to act in some definite way. For example, if citizens of a certain nation have the legal right to marry, then there will be (1) other identifiable individuals or groups (e.g., judges) who have (2) identifiable duties to act (e.g., to officiate at weddings). In what follows I will call the members of the first group "the *who*" since they are the people who have a certain set of obligations, and I will call the obligations which they have "the *how*" since these obligations specify the way in which "the *who*" are expected to act. Under these conditions it would be correct to say that the citizens of that nation have a *valid claim* (which is Feinberg's preferred description of a right) against any parties opposed to their plan to marry (such as a jilted lover). They may justifiably demand that those opposing parties behave accordingly. In other words, regardless of their feelings the other parties owe their cooperation (or at least non-interference) to these and any other citizens who also have the right to marry.

However, Feinberg argues, when we come to *human rights* things are more complicated, since there may not be any identifiable parties who have corresponding identifiable duties. As he puts it,

> Manifesto writers ... who seem to identify needs, or at least basic needs, with what they call "human rights" are more properly described, I think, as urging upon the world community the moral principle that all basic human needs ought to be recognized as claims (in the customary prima facie sense) worthy of sympathy and serious consideration right now, even though, in many cases, they cannot yet plausibly be treated as valid claims, that is, as grounds of other people's duties.[3]

That is, such claims, even though frequently articulated in the language of rights, should not be considered rights-claims. Strictly speaking, these moral claims should be expressed in some other terms. What is entailed by thinking of these cases as rights-claims does not in fact apply, Feinberg argues, since there are no identifiable individuals or groups who have corresponding identifiable duties to act.

Feinberg does not have much more to say about this argument, which follows directly from what he says that we mean when we say "so-and-so has a right." However, the relevant components of Feinberg's analysis of what "having a right" means are widely accepted as correct, whether or not they are worded in exactly the same way, and so it is hard to deny what seems to be the clear implication of this account of what "having a right" means: namely, that many so-called human rights are not really rights at all.

As was mentioned above, Feinberg is not challenging the moral importance of important human needs, especially basic needs, wherever they are going unfulfilled. He almost immediately follows the passage just quoted by saying:

> Natural needs are real claims, if only upon hypothetical future beings not yet in existence. I accept the moral principle that to have an unfulfilled need is to have a kind of claim against the world, even if against no one in particular.... A person in need ... is always "in a position" to make a claim, even if there is no one in the corresponding position to do anything about it.[4]

When, as he puts it, "there is no one in the corresponding position to do anything about it," it would seem that moral claims of this sort cannot properly be rights-claims, and they should not be called rights. However, Feinberg admits:

> For all of that, I still have a certain sympathy with the manifesto writers, and am even willing to speak of a special "manifesto sense" of "right," in which a right need not be correlated with another's duty.... [W]hen manifesto writers speak of [such needs-based claims] as if they are already actual rights, they are easily forgiven, for this is

but a powerful way of expressing the conviction that they ought to be recognized by states as potential rights and consequently as determinants of present aspirations and guides to present policies. That usage, I think, is a valid exercise of rhetorical license.[5]

Nevertheless it remains true for Feinberg that making such a right-claim must be viewed as at best what he calls an "exercise of rhetorical license." Since we cannot identify who has the corresponding obligations or what kinds of acting or refraining are required, it would seem that these claims cannot be genuine right-claims.

There are a number of thinkers, most notably Onora O'Neill,[6] who have not been as willing as Feinberg to grant this rhetorical license. Thus James Griffin was able to say in 2008: "Many rights can be, and already are, demoted to the status of mere aspirations rather than rights proper (e.g., the 'right' to peace); [and] a pejorative term has been coined for them: 'manifesto rights.'"[7] In other words, Feinberg's answer to the meaning question has apparently had the opposite effect, leading other rights thinkers to reject his own attempt to restore some status to such claims. Some of these thinkers, including O'Neill, do agree with Feinberg that strong moral claims (even when they are not rights-claims) can be made by and for persons who have unmet basic needs, but other thinkers do not. However, the point here is that Feinberg's original argument has not been seriously challenged: when it comes to such basic claims, we cannot identify just who has duties to act nor how they should do so.

At this point I should declare my own view, which is the thesis of the present essay. It is that if the meaning of a rights-claim is examined more carefully, it will be clear that the kinds of rights-claims that Feinberg has called "manifesto rights" do in fact imply identifiable obligations to act (the *how*) on the part of identifiable parties (the *who*) and in fact that, in a very important sense, all of us are involved.

Separating the Meaning Conditions from Truth Conditions

Talk of rights is all around us and we all know how to formulate sentences using these concepts. However, to determine if a piece of talk about rights is genuinely informative about what ought or ought not to be done, and by whom, it is necessary to ask how well-reasoned rights-based moral or ethical thinking works, and for many people the answer to this question is far from clear. This is not surprising, given how much scholarly ink has been spilled trying to get a dependable definition of a right or, what is the same question in different words, an answer to the meaning-question about rights-claims. In light of so much spilled ink, the British legal scholar H.L.A. Hart proposed in his inaugural lecture at Oxford back in 1953 that thinkers set aside their efforts to define "a right" and—to paraphrase Hart—instead ask two questions that can be worded as: "What needs to be the case for a typical sentence claiming that someone has a right, that is, a rights-claim, to be meaningful?" and "What needs to be the case for a typical sentence making a rights-claim to be true?"[8]

Let us begin with the meaning-question. Feinberg's and most other scholars' answer to the meaning-question for rights-claims can be summarized as follows. For a rights-claim to be meaningful (i.e., to make good sense and thereby be at all useful in communicating about what ought or ought not to be done), it must be the case that:

1. There is someone (an individual or a group of persons), A, who has the right;
2. There is some determinate party (an individual or a group of persons), B, who has an obligation to act or refrain from acting in some way in relation to A;
3. How B ought to act or refrain is determinable and possible for B; and
4. B's obligation to act or refrain has high moral priority–typically, the highest moral priority.

In Gregory Vlastos's phrase, B's obligation "takes precedence"; that is, it has greater moral priority than any other moral consideration that is relevant to B's acting or refraining in the situation,[9] or as Ronald Dworkin famously put it, rights-claims function in moral discourse as moral "trumps."[10]

Obviously it is the second requirement (the *who*) and the third requirement (the *how*) that are most relevant to the distinction that Feinberg makes between genuine rights and manifesto rights as well as to the debate among thinkers about whether so-called human rights are genuine rights in the first place. For example, consider Feinberg's and O'Neill's view that the claim that every human has a right not to be tortured is almost certainly a meaningful rights-claim. It seems clear that the *who* in such a claim is every other individual and group capable of torturing another human, and it is arguably possible to determine with sufficient clarity when an action is to be counted as torturing someone, that is, the *how*. However, if a rights-claims leaves the *who* or the *how* undetermined, then for Feinberg and O'Neill and others, the moral claims involved in the situation are not genuine rights-claims, even though they might be fully morally defensible—that is, both meaningful and true—in terms of other moral or ethical concepts.

Once we know that a particular rights-claim is meaningful in the sense that it fulfills the four meaning-conditions just identified, then we can ask if that rights-claim is also true (rather than false). It is taken for granted throughout this discussion that rights-claims that are not meaningful are *neither true nor false*. That is one reason why the claim that many human-rights-claims are not meaningful is so important. If they are not meaningful, they cannot be either true or false. That is one reason why the claim that many human-rights-claims are not meaningful is so important. If they are not meaningful, they cannot be either true or false.

Because of the special moral priority that is part of the meaning of a rights-claim (meaning-condition No. 4 above), there is a tendency on the part of those who hear a rights-claim, and especially of those who make a rights-claim, to assume that it must be true. This assumption is a mistake (though it has obvious rhetorical force) because many of the rights-claims made in our daily lives are meaningful, but false. Consider this example, taken from a local sports page the day after a certain high school football team lost in the state's semi-finals. The team's coach was quoted as saying: "Even though our school's football team lost the semi-final game, they played well enough that they have a right to play in the championship game."

This rights-claim is clearly meaningful. We know who has the right (the coach's team), who has the obligation (the managers of the tournament), and how those parties are supposedly obliged to act (put the coach's team in the championship game) and to refrain (leave all but one other team out of the game). Yet this rights-claim is clearly false because the truth-conditions regarding rights-claims in the finals of a football tournament are such that only teams who have won their semi-final game may compete in the championship game.

This happens to be an example of rights-claims whose truth-conditions are tied to the existence of some sort of social system that has been accepted by all of the participants. In this case, the rights claims are based on the accepted procedures by which football teams are selected to play in championship games. Rights-claims whose truth-conditions are tied to the existence of an accepted social system are known in the rights literature as "conventional rights," and there are many kinds of conventional rights because there are many kinds of social systems, large and small, in which rights-claims can be meaningfully made.

However, there is another kind of rights-claim in which the truth-conditions do not depend in any way on the socially accepted standard of any society or other social group. These are claims about human rights. This feature of human-rights-claims is the main reason that determining the truth or falsity of a human-rights-claim can be so difficult and even contentious. Those who hold that a particular human-rights-claim is true also hold that its truth is independent of anyone's choosing or agreeing that there be such a right. In short, its truth is in some way part of the moral nature of things.

To sum up so far: In general, there are two kinds of arguments that have been offered in the literature on human rights in order to support the idea that a particular human-rights-claim is true (or false). One kind focuses on characteristics common to all humans, and the other on needs common to all humans.[11] In fact, most of the literature of human rights has focused on determining when and why certain human-rights-claims are true (or false) and has simply presupposed that the human-rights-claims being considered are meaningful. In other words, the arguments by Feinberg, O'Neill, and others that many human-rights-claims do not fulfill the meaning-conditions for rights-claims (and therefore are neither true nor false) have not been very carefully examined.

Two Partial Responses to Feinberg

When Feinberg and O'Neill, as well as many other rights theorists, have looked for what H.L.A. Hart called "typical contexts where these words are at work,"[12] they have taken the typical rights-claim that we find at work in national legal systems as the paradigm for all rights-claims. For this reason, it is perhaps to be expected that they would associate meaningfulness with a high level of precision regarding the *who* and the *how* of rights-claims. If a legal-rights-claim is made, but it is not clear within the relevant legal system who has a legal duty (the *who*) or how this party is required to act or refrain (the *how*), then typically nothing significant will happen until such questions are resolved in some way, usually by the courts. In practice, if a court were to determine that the implications of a particular legal-rights-claim were not resolvable, most persons describing the situation would say that the claimant did not have the relevant right (i.e., that the rights-claim was false). But the correct description of the court's decision would be that the rights-claim proved to be meaningless rather than false, for the problem was that it did not fulfill all the conditions of being a meaningful rights claim, and meaningless rights-claims are neither true nor false.

But are Feinberg *et al.* correct in taking legal-rights-claims as the model of "a typical sentence claiming that someone has a right"? There is another fairly distinct kind of socially accepted standard besides legal standards, and this means that there are two fairly distinct kinds of conventional rights-claims.[13] Only one of these is well represented by legal-rights-claims, so an effort to understand what rights-claims mean that focuses only on legal-rights-claims may be missing something important.

Many familiar systems of socially accepted standards (hereafter, "SAS's") can be called "formal" systems of SAS's for at least three reasons: they are characterized by explicit and often very detailed descriptions of offices and roles, there are explicit descriptions of many of the behaviors to be undertaken or avoided by persons or groups in these offices and roles, and there are often explicit mechanisms for adding to or amending already existing SAS's that make up the system. Legal systems are obviously like this. However, there are many other, equally familiar but often less obvious, systems of SAS's that could be called "informal" because they lack such explicit descriptions of roles and behavior. They frequently have few or no mechanisms for adding to or amending the existing SAS's besides the mechanisms of mutual agreement/acceptance by which they were originally created, and they are frequently composed solely of SAS's directly accepted by the relevant group without formal procedures.

Since a legal system is a formal system, legal-rights-claims do typically identify a definite *who* that is claimed to have obligations and a definite *how* that the party in question ought to observe. Thus it is reasonable that Feinberg and other scholars who take legal-rights-claims as their primary examples of rights-claims have held that a determinate *who* and a determinate *how* are necessary features of a meaningful rights-claim. But now consider rights-claims that are made in an informal conventional system of SAS's, where the basis of rights-claims has been established informally by the members of some group. Suppose my neighbor and I agree to split evenly the cost of the food that I will purchase so that we can together contribute it to the neighborhood block party. While formal legal property rights could be invoked if my neighbor does not pay me for his share, the claim "I have a right to half of the cost" could easily and naturally be understood to be a meaningful rights-claim simply because he and I made an (informal) agreement.

Notice that our agreement might not have included any details about when or how the payment of my neighbor's share would take place or by what means (cash, check, barter, etc.). This ambiguity could make it difficult to determine whether at a particular point in time my rights-claim is correct. I may have thought he was agreeing to pay me as soon as I purchased the food or at least before the day was out, but he might have assumed that I understood that he would be repaying me much later because earlier in the day, when food for the block party was not yet on our minds, he had happened to mention to me quite explicitly that he was presently short of cash. Given this shortfall in our communication about the informal rights established between us, a general statement that "I have a right to half of the cost" might be true, but it would be doubtful whether I have a specific right to be paid by the end of the day. That is, indefiniteness about precisely *how* the neighbor ought to act (or refrain) is certainly important in determining the truth or falsity of a more precise version of "I have a right to half of the cost," but it does not challenge the meaningfulness of this rights-claim as general statement of my rights-claim.

Similar ambiguities about the *who* could also exist without the general rights-claims being meaningless. It would not be unusual for the agreement between me and my neighbor to have been understood as an agreement between our two families, not only if this understanding was explicitly stated when my neighbor and I made our agreement, but also if, though not explicitly mentioned, it happened to be part of the way our two families or families in our neighborhood typically interact in situations of this kind. If it was clearly understood by both parties to be an agreement between our families, then it would clearly be false for me to say "I have a right to half of the cost" if my neighbor's wife had already given the money to my wife, and it would be false even if I did not know they had taken care of it.

However, this kind of indefiniteness about the *who* would not make the general rights-claim, "I (or we) have a right to half of the cost," meaningless. In in this way, in many informal social situations, the truth or falsity of more narrowly worded informal conventional rights-claims may be difficult to determine because of unresolved ambiguities about the *who* and/or *how*. Even so, this kind of indefiniteness does not necessarily render meaningless more generally worded rights-claims about the same matter. In practice, when such ambiguities arise and need to be resolved in order that the generally worded rights-claim be fulfilled, the parties involved engage in conversation, examining various combinations of *who* and *how* until agreement is reached about a concrete method of fulfilling the right. Frequently, these conversations involve efforts to identify a method which, among the available alternatives, maximizes the values that are relevant to the situation, or other moral or ethical considerations may complement or override such value-maximizing efforts in some situations. But the fact that participants in such situations typically proceed to resolve what is indefinite about the *who* or the *how* in order to be sure that the general rights-claim is properly acted upon is surely evidence that they did not consider the general rights claim to be meaningless until these matters became definite.

These facts about informal conventional rights-claims do not imply that rights-claims in informal social settings are invariably meaningful. If my neighbor tells me he will pay his share when his son, George, returns from getting some cash at the cash station and I agree specifically to this arrangement, but he has in fact no son George, then our agreement has not established a meaningful rights-claim for me to be paid. I might have a meaningful, and possibly true, rights-claim to half the cost of the food in light of other considerations that are relevant to the situation. However, a rights-claim grounded specifically on our having agreed to something that is impossible of fulfillment would be a meaningless rights-claim. Since Feinberg himself seems to hold that informal conventional rights can be meaningful (even though what he says about the formal/ informal distinction is not easy to decipher),[14] it is at least plausible that our ability to give general answers to the *who* and the *how* questions is sufficient. This seems to be what Griffin is proposing when he argues, in a section titled "Can There Be Rights Without Identifiable Duty-Bearers?" that a rights-claim is meaningful as long as we can describe who the duty-bearer would be.[15]

A second, related kind of response to Feinberg is offered by Griffin in his *On Human Rights* when he responds to a similar argument by O'Neill.[16] Griffin argues on the basis of concrete examples that, for many human-rights-claims like those named in the United Nations *Declaration on Human Rights,* the *who,* namely the relevant institutions, offices, and roles within national legal systems and NGO's—and thus the groups and persons who fill the relevant offices, roles, etc.—who have the obligations implied by the rights-claim can indeed be identified by examining the particular kind of right that is claimed. He argues similarly that the *how,* that is, the relevant actions, will be determinable in any concrete case. In other words, Griffin's argument is that conversations such as those which (as we saw above) can resolve indeterminateness about the *who* and the *how* are no less possible in the case of human-rights-claims, contrary to the view of those who, following Feinberg, believe the who and/or the *how* of such claims are simply not determinable.

If this argument were generalized, its conclusion would be that it is in fact possible to identify the *who* and the *how* for all the well-known human-rights-claims once we know the particular kind of right that is claimed and the respective positions of relevant parties in relation to the rights-bearer. Unfortunately for Griffin's argument, it is hard to see how this kind of analysis could in fact be completed for each of the human-rights-claims that are currently made regarding complex issues such as people's unmet basic needs around the globe. In many cases, Feinberg and others would argue, patterns of international distribution, regional and local social systems, as well as a simple lack of knowledge on the part of relevant parties in the developed world mean that no one really knows *how* the needs could be met by any real (i.e., non-imaginary) *who* now or in the foreseeable future.

A similar point holds regarding the *who*. Although Griffin says that a rights-claim is meaningful as long as we can describe who the duty-bearer would be, Feinberg and O'Neill could reply that he is only presuming that such a person could exist, and that this presumption needs to be supported. Indeed, although at one point Griffin himself says "The acceptable requirement of claimability is that the duty-bearers be specifiable, not that they exist," only two sentences later he qualifies his own conclusion by adding "... if there might eventually be some [definite duty-bearer]."[17] Conversely, in light of these arguments Feinberg and O'Neill may need to grant that for at least some well-known human-rights-claims—here understood as general rights-claims analogous to those discussed above in connection with informal conventional systems—the *who* and the *how* could be described in such a way that these are indeed meaningful rights-claims. They may need to grant that more human-rights-claims are meaningful than their arguments to date suggest. They may also need to admit that they have focused too closely on the high level of precision that is typical of the more technical genre of legal-rights-claims, as well as the fact that ambiguity about the specifics of *who* and *how* does not automatically render a general human-rights-claim meaningless. However, these adjustments of the Feinberg-O'Neill position do not dissolve their argument. There clearly seem to be human-rights-claims that cannot be fulfilled now or in the foreseeable future. If Feinberg and O'Neill's answer to the meaning-question about rights-claims is correct and complete, then human-rights-claims of this sort would not be meaningful. Although they are often called human rights, such claims would only be "manifesto rights"—to be called rights only by rhetorical license, if at all—and they should not be considered rights-claims in any literal sense.

So Feinberg's original challenge remains standing: Is a human-rights-claim meaningful if it simply cannot be fulfilled now or in the foreseeable future? If the correct answer to this question is "Yes, these human-rights-claims are meaningful!"—as most people who talk about human rights and make human-rights-claims clearly believe—then something important is missing in the conversation. We need a better, fuller answer to the meaning-question about rights-claims that Feinberg and O'Neill and many other rights scholars have defended.

To Whom Are Rights-Claims Addressed?

To see what is missing in these philosophers' and political theorists' answers to the meaning-question of rights-claims, we need to ask a question about rights-claims that has received very little attention: To whom are rights-claims addressed? One of the most frequently cited contributions to our understanding of rights in Feinberg's essay, "The Nature and Value of Rights," is his eloquent argument that rights-claims are distinctive in comparison with other kinds of claims about what ought and ought not to be done. One view of the distinctiveness of rights-claims focuses on their having special moral priority in comparison with other kinds of moral or ethical considerations, and that priority was identified above as the fourth necessary characteristic of a meaningful rights-claim.[18] In fact, since rights-claims can conflict with one another and still be meaningful, it is doubtful that mere structural priority is necessary for a rights-claim to be meaningful.[19]

In "The Nature and Value of Rights," Feinberg offers a robust description of the special moral priority of rights-claims and of what makes them distinctive among judgments about what ought and ought not to be done. He proposes that "the most conspicuous difference [between rights and other ways of judging what ought or ought not to be done] ... has something to do with the activity of claiming. ... [T]here is no doubt that their characteristic use and that for which they are distinctively well suited is to be claimed, demanded, affirmed, insisted upon [since] it is claiming that gives rights their special moral significance."[20]

Rights-claims are distinctive, Feinberg is saying, because they are not simply theoretical judgments offered for other theorists' consideration regarding what ought or ought not to be done by some anonymous agent. Right-claims should have theoretical underpinnings but they are also claims, demands, or insistings. In other words, a rights-claim is made within a special relationship with others, one that allows for claiming, demanding, and insisting, as well as theoretical discussions of what ought and ought not to be done. To whom, then, are rights-claims addressed?

Since there are two distinct kinds of rights-claims—conventional-rights-claims and human-rights-claims—we need to ask this "Who is addressed?" question for each kind of rights-claim. In doing so it will become clear that in both types of rights-claims, those who are addressed are not only persons in clearly identifiable social roles or offices but also a much larger set of persons that I will simply call the "Rest of Us."

Let us begin with formal conventional rights, as Feinberg and O'Neill do, and in particular with legal-rights-claims (as they also do). When someone violates one of my legal rights, to whom do I address my claim about required acting and refraining? Feinberg and O'Neill's answer to the meaning-question about rights-claims focuses on the most obvious answer to this question, but it is not the complete answer—and so their response to the meaning-question about rights-claims is incomplete.

For example, if my car is stolen I would (in an ideal case) assert my rights-claim first to the thief, citing his or her obligation to refrain from taking my car in the first place. I would also assert my claim to the police and eventually to the courts, citing their obligation to try to identify the thief, charge him or her with violating my legal property rights, etc. However, these are not the only parties whom I would be addressing with my legal-rights-claim. For instance, suppose that my neighbor happened to observe the thief at work. In that case, I would also assert my neighbor's obligation to assist me in providing this information to the police. I would address any other persons who saw the event or who in other ways could assist in the recovery of my car or the apprehension of the thief, and this list could easily include distant strangers who simply suspected that a certain car might be stolen, and so on. Moreover, my tacit claim that others should not take my legal property is addressed not only to the thief but also to every other member of the same legal system. Indeed, there is only one clear limit to membership in the group of persons whom I would be addressing in my legal-rights-claim: it does not include persons who are not members of the same legal system. (Even so, although they would not have any legal obligations to help me recover my car, they might have other morally relevant obligations to do so.)

However, what about persons who are members of the same legal system but have no connection whatsoever to any aspect of the theft? The most relevant question here is whether anyone actually fits this description. For instance, suppose that the police or the courts failed in their socially accepted roles in relation to this theft, and did so for reasons of incompetence or deliberate failure to perform their roles properly. I would surely claim that this is a violation of my legal rights regarding my car (and probably of other legal rights as well) and I would call on all my fellow citizens to take action to correct the situation. In practice, of course, this particular articulation of the matter would likely come later in time, but it is already implicit in my original legal-rights-claim.

That is, when I make any legal-rights-claim, I am addressing every member of my legal system to support the proper working of the legal system regarding, for example, property relations and the system's ways of dealing with violators. I am claiming that they all ought to act and/or refrain in whatever ways are relevant, depending on each one's position and opportunities in relation to the situation. In other words, the only persons whom I am not addressing in my legal-rights-claim are those who are not members of the same legal system.

It is not difficult to generalize from this example. Anyone who is a member of a formal social system that includes rights and who makes a system-based rights-claim is in fact addressing every other member of that social system, whether we are talking about a legal system or a formal institution or organization of some other sort, large or small. When I make a formal-SAS-based rights-claim, I am addressing every other member of that social system and am saying that, because I have this right, they ought to act and refrain in such a way that my right is not violated in the first place and, if it is violated, they ought to act and refrain in ways that contribute to the proper (as defined within the system) resolution of the matter. What precise actions and refrainings these obligations will require of a given person or group will depend on their various roles within the system and their particular connection to the matter.

In other words, besides the most obvious answers to the *who* question (namely those answers that give legal rights the appearance of precision that Feinberg and O'Neill claim is a meaning-condition for rights-claims), legal-rights-claims entail obligations for a far larger *who* than Feinberg and O'Neill consider. This point holds for all formal social systems that include rights. In other words, for every formal social system that includes rights, a description of the meaning-conditions of any member's rights-claims within that system, whether describable or not, will always be incomplete unless it also includes the Rest of Us.

Furthermore, this point holds for informal conventional rights-claims. When a person makes a rights-claim, that claim is addressed to every participant in the relevant social system. However, since we are thinking here about an informal social system, it is often more difficult to tell who are members of the system than in the case of a formal system, if only because one of the marks of a formal social system is that it has fairly precise criteria for determining membership. In the case of an informal social system, however, the criterion of membership is the individual's exhibiting a pattern of acceptance of whatever norms of behavior, for example, have been mutually accepted. Unfortunately, what counts in practice as "exhibiting a pattern of acceptance" is not easily described and this can create ambiguity about who is a member and who is not, especially at the "edges" of an informal social group.[21] Nevertheless, for the same kinds of reasons just explained in the case of a formal conventional system, it follows that a description of the meaning-conditions of any member's rights-claims within an informal system will nevertheless be incomplete until it also includes the Rest of Us, that is, all who are members of that informal social system. (This point holds regardless of whether a precisely identifiable set of persons is currently part of the answer to the *who* question.)

Moreover, as was the case with formal conventional rights-claims, although a rights-claim based on informal SAS's is addressed to all who are members of the relevant system, it is not addressed to persons who are not members of the system (remembering that, especially at the "edges," determining who is not a member of an informal system may be complex). Consider, for example, a social system consisting in just two persons. Suppose I invite a friend to dinner in honor of the friend's birthday and we agree to meet at the restaurant at 6:00. We have created a social system regarding our actions and, assuming the matter is morally significant enough, I could meaningfully claim to have a right to my friend's timely presence.[22] Now suppose that my friend fails to show up and I complain to someone at the restaurant that my right has been violated. This third party could reasonably say, "I feel sorry for you for being stood up, but whether you have a rights-claim or not is between you and your friend. As a rights-claim, it cannot be addressed to me." In other words, my conventional rights-claim involves only the two of us and can therefore be meaningfully addressed only to my friend.

Can the same thing be said about human-rights-claims? To whom are human-rights-claims addressed? As with conventional-rights-claims, there may be human-rights-claims that are addressed initially to persons closely connected with the claimant, such as local officials or regional or national assistance programs. However, if these fall short, and the claimants consciously address their claims more broadly, does the fact that their claim is now definitely addressed to a larger audience mean that the person is making a different rights claim? Suppose we ask this question of persons who make human-rights-claims in the midst of wars, famines, epidemics, and other conditions profoundly threatening to human life. Their answer would surely be, "No, my human-rights-claim was addressed to you all along, but I turned to them for help first for obvious practical reasons." In short, human-rights-claims are claims on anyone anywhere who can positively impact a claimant's situation in any way. Therefore, there is little reason to think that human-rights-claims are different from conventional rights-claims in this respect. It is part of the meaning of every rights-claim that its *who* always includes the Rest of Us, whether this is explicitly mentioned or initially goes unnoticed. So the remaining question about the *who* for human-rights-claims is: Who should be considered the Rest of Us when the rights-claim is a human-rights-claim? And the answer is: *All of us.* But is this a determinate *who?*

The heart of the Feinberg/O'Neill objection to the meaningfulness of most human rights claims is that the *who* is not determinate. Before proceeding, therefore, it is important to ask whether they would consider the *who* that has just been identified—viz., the Rest of Us, which is all of us—to be determinate. However, Feinberg and O'Neill along with many other thinkers have held that, at least regarding the human right not to be tortured, a *who* consisting of every other capable human being is considered to be determinate. Thus, they can have no objection based on determinateness to the current proposal that, whether or not any person or persons might also be able to be specified more precisely, human-rights-claims are always about what the Rest of Us owe the rights-bearer. The determinate *who* for human rights claims is always: "all of us, every capable human being."

This conclusion about who has the obligation for human-rights-claims also provides an answer to the question: "To whom are human-rights-claims addressed?" Just as in the case of a legal-rights-claim when my car is stolen, I will first address my claim to the persons most likely to be able to help, namely the police and courts, but if they fail me, my claim has already implied that the rest of the legal community has obligations to assist me. Those whose human rights are not fulfilled may turn first to those who fill relevant conventional roles and offices, but if these fail them, or if they know of none to turn to, their human-rights-claim has already been addressed to the Rest of Us and it already implies obligations on us to act and/or refrain. And this takes us to the question of the *how* of human-rights-claims.

The *How* of Human Rights Claims: What the Rest of Us Should Do

How should we respond to human-rights-claims? To begin to answer this question, let us first return to the topic of formal legal-rights-claims and reflect a bit further on the *how* question that Feinberg and O'Neill have described. It is true that many of the actings and refrainings that are required by citizens' legal-rights-claims are typically identified in the descriptions of legal roles and offices, and that these in turn are descriptions of various tasks to be done, goals to be reached, and the like. That is, they consist in determinate kinds of actings and refrainings, as Feinberg and O'Neill clearly imply. However, upon reflection it is clear that this portrayal of the *how* implied by a legal-rights-claim is actually incomplete: it lacks the precision that our authors attribute to it, and it does so in two ways. First, as mentioned in our examination of the *who* that constitutes the background of legal-rights-claims, there are many, indeed very many, people who have obligations implied by my legal-rights-claim besides those people who play formally defined roles in the legal system. This means that no matter how carefully the formal roles are described, those descriptions would be only a small part of what could be said about the *how* in the course of identifying the implicit actings and refrainings that are required by my legal-rights-claim.

Second, even for those fulfilling a formal social role or office, determining what they ought to do or not do always involves judgments whose content cannot be completely predicted, if only because they depend on the discretion of the role- or office-holder. This holds even within very precise formal systems, legal and otherwise,[23] as well as within most informal systems, especially those made up of large numbers of persons. So again, if the criterion is typical sentences claiming that someone has a conventional right, whether formal or informal, the argument offered by Feinberg and O'Neill in fact misrepresents the degree of precision to be found in what rights-claims imply about the *how*.

But if the precision about the *how* that Feinberg and O'Neill presume is in fact not part of the implications of typical rights-claims, how then can those who have obligations figure out what they should do? If we look at conventional rights-claims, the general answer is the one offered above, namely that my conventional-rights-claim is addressed to every other member of the relevant social system and asserts that, because I have this right, they ought to act in such a way that my right is not violated in the first place. If it is violated, they ought to act and refrain in ways that contribute to the proper (as defined within the system) resolution of the matter. The rest of the answer will depend on the particular rights-claim being made, the social roles and offices (if any) that are relevant to it, and the other ways in which other members of the relevant system are connected to whatever the rights-claim is about.

In his book *Basic Rights*,[24] Henry Shue provides a useful general description of the *how* that is implied and demanded of everyone in human-rights-claims:

> Duty 1. To refrain from violating
> Duty 2. To protect from violations
>> Duty 2a. by enforcing Duty #1
>> Duty 2b. by designing institutions that avoid the creation of strong incentives to violate Duty #1
> Duty 3. To aid those whose human rights are at significant risk of or are already being violated, and
>> Duty 3a. who are one's special responsibility

> Duty 3b. who are victims of social failures in
> people's performance of Duties 1, 2a, and
> 2b
>
> Duty 3c. and who are victims of natural
> disasters.[25]

Obviously, as already noted, there may be persons or groups in offices or other social roles in the area, region, or nation of someone who makes a human-rights-claim. These persons or groups are readily identifiable as having duties in one or more of Shue's categories. In addition, since the *who* that are addressed by human-rights-claims are all other humans capable of responding in any relevant way, there may be persons or groups in offices or other social roles within NGO's or in other nations who are readily identifiable as having such duties. In any event, the proposal offered here is that the Rest of Us have duties as well. What then do these duties look like?

To answer this question, I will speak in the first person about responses to human rights claims. If I, the author of this essay, am one of the *who* to whom such claims are addressed, then what is the implicit *how* regarding the actions (which include refrainings) that I should take in response to the human-rights-claim of someone living in, say, one of the impoverished nations of what was once called the Third World or in one of the places around the globe that have been ravaged by war or violence?

I am a professor of philosophy in a large university in the United States. Any connection I actually have with an unfortunate distant person whose human-rights-claim I am now trying to understand is very indirect. It is mediated by my own nation's government, whose relevant officers and offices are not likely to be directly responsive to my concerns, as well as by various NGO's that I can contact more or less directly in order to offer financial and perhaps volunteer support. In addition, especially if I contact an appropriate NGO, I might have some impact, especially if I have relevant skills that fit with the organization's activities. For starters, then, the distant person's human-rights-claim seems to imply that—if his or her situation is in fact one in which basic needs are not being met due to natural disaster or social failures in people's performance of Shue's Duties #1, #2A, or #2B—then I ought to be trying to offer aid (Duty #3) via financial and/or possibly volunteer support of the work of some appropriate NGO or governmental office. Of course, the question immediately arises about how much such support I am obliged to provide in the course of addressing this person's human-rights-claim. In fact, this question will arise regarding any obligations that might be implied for me in this human-rights-claim, and so I will examine it in the next section. There are, however, many potential NGO's and governmental offices that might serve as intermediaries for my efforts to provide aid to this person, and it is reasonable to assume that they will differ greatly in efficiency and in their sensitivity to Duty #2B. Both my duty to aid (Duty #3) and the obligation that all of us have to fulfill Duty #2B imply that I have an obligation to choose an intermediary that is not likely to be violating Duty #2B with my contributed resources and whose operations will make the best use of my contributed resources (Duty #3) to improve this rights-bearer's situation. Obviously, responding to this duty requires some effort on my part to become informed about potential intermediaries in these respects. Just how much effort is required will depend on how great the risks of inefficiency and violations of Duty #2B are among the potential intermediaries known to me.

This much may seem obvious, but there are at least three other, more problematic connections between myself and the person whose rights-claim I am trying to sort out. One of these connections derives from my status as a citizen and voter. My national government, and possibly also state and local governmental offices, often engage in actions and follows policies that have the potential not only to create incentives for various parties to violate Duty #1 but also to create disincentives to enforce Duty #1. As a philosophy professor, my direct influence on such governmental bodies and offices is slight at best. However, as a citizen, I could voice my concerns to these offices directly if there was reason to think such efforts might have some proportionate impact. In any case, I am a voter, and these duties imply an obligation on my part to employ my votes, insofar as relevant information is accessible to me, to ensure that these governmental bodies and offices act in accord with Duty #1 and both parts of Duty #2, as well as to respond to Duty #3 as efficiently as possible. I am also a consumer. The ways in which entrepreneurial organizations can violate Duty #1 and Duty #2 are myriad, and the relevant systems of manufacture, distribution, and finance are so intricate and interconnected that my ability to favor organizations who do not violate these duties and to avoid commercial support of those who do is very limited. However, as these duties are incumbent on all of us, I clearly do have some obligations to the person whose human-rights-claims I am imagining here, such as the obligation to seek out relevant information and direct my commercial transactions as efficiently as I can toward organizations that take these duties seriously.

Finally, and most importantly from the point of view of long-term impact, I am an educator. I have many kinds of obligations to those whom I teach. I am clearly obligated, in my conventional role as a professor, to guide my students in learning about the real state of the world, including the real situations of persons whose basic needs are not fulfilled. In particular, as a teacher of ethics and social philosophy, I owe it to my students to help them understand that meaningful rights-claims are not necessarily true rights-claims and to help them learn how to judge when a meaningful human-rights-claim is true and when it is false. My students have these conventional expectations of me, some of which are based on their own human rights. As a teacher, I also seem to have still another obligation to the unfortunate person "out there" who is the source the human-rights-claim that I have been considering, namely my professional obligation to explain this person's situation to my students in the course of teaching classes on ethics or social justice. And so forth. All these are ways in which, over the long run, the duties implied in this distant person's clear and meaningful rights-claims can be fulfilled. In short, it would be a mistake to claim that in my role and office as a teacher, I have no significant connection to this person's human-rights-claims.

In sum, although this listing of obligations is clearly incomplete and based on a single example, it remains true that, in order to adequately understand the implications of a meaningful human-rights-claim, we need to identify the ways in which each of us is connected, sometimes directly but always indirectly, to the makers of human-rights-claims. Examples of obligations such as these can help identify the kinds of questions each of us needs to ask, guided for example by Shue's general list of categories. Each of us owes it to the person making human-rights-claims to ask such questions and to work out how to answer them appropriately.

Admittedly, sorting out the details of the *how* will almost always prove very complicated, and the question of "how much" must still be addressed. Even so, it is simply false to say that the *who* and the *how* that are implied in a typical human-rights-claim are so hopelessly indeterminate that most human-rights-claims are not really meaningful. Whether or not a particular case involves readily identifiable individuals or holders of offices or social roles, every meaningful human-rights-claim invariably includes all the Rest of Us among those who have obligations to respond in some way to a claimant's call for help. Among the duties that follow from human rights claims is the obligation to make as careful a judgment as possible about how we should proceed. And that is something very definite.

How Much of the *How*?

What has been said in the last two sections about what a meaningful human-rights-claim implies for the Rest of Us, gives rise to a further question: How much? How much are the Rest of Us obligated to do in response to the meaningful human-rights-claims of others that, on careful consideration, we judge are not only meaningful but also true?[26] How much financial assistance does a human-rights-claim imply that each of us owes in fulfillment of Duty #3? How much volunteer service? How much attention to monitoring governmental agencies and entrepreneurial organizations in order not to support actions on their part that violate Duty #1 and Duty #2? And so on. There are no answers to this question that are not highly dependent on the situation and reasonable opportunities of the person answering it.[27]

With regard to Shue's Duty #1, it seems clear that a human-rights-claim implies that all the Rest of Us are obligated to refrain from directly depriving any other person of things about which they can make meaningful and true human-rights-claims. With regard to Duty #1, then, it may seem that the proper answer to the "How much?" question must be "Whatever it takes." But even this oversimplifies matters. There are some situations in which the actions or refrainings necessary to avoid the violation of one party's human rights will very likely violate those of another party. An obvious example would be the use of defensive violence to protect a third party from serious harm.

Most often in the lives of the readers of this essay, however, such conflicts will arise regarding the indirect effects of our actions and refrainings on persons whose human rights are at risk. For example, for the vast majority of people with some relevant surplus of resources, determining how much financial assistance (or time and effort as a volunteer) to offer in response to Duty #3 or how much sacrifice of financial efficiency and of time and effort to spend in response to Duties #2A and #2B in one's role as citizen/voter or as a consumer involve weighing the indirect effects of our actions and refrainings on competing human-rights-claims of different parties.

Two kinds of considerations are especially relevant here. First, from the point of view of a person whose human rights are not fulfilled, it is reasonable to expect that every human-rights-claim takes absolute precedence over every other kind of moral consideration that might be relevant to the person's situation. Human-rights-claims are often claims about the situation of someone who lacks what is necessary to be at least minimally effective as a human being. They are about, as Shue puts it, "the morality of the depths;" since they are about "preventing or alleviating helplessness."[28] For anyone who is neither a saint nor a fool, filling such essential needs is a necessary precondition for pursuing other values, conforming to other principles, or following other ideals. This ranking of goals and outcomes suggests that human-rights-claims obligations have greater moral weight than those of other kinds of rights, that what Shue calls "cultural enrichment" ranks below both of these, and that each in turn morally outweighs what he calls "preference satisfaction."[29]

On the other hand, many of the decisions we make about the use of our material resources, time, and effort are directly or indirectly connected to the human rights of persons for whom we are responsible in various ways. That is, while Shue's Duty #3A—to aid in the fulfillment of the human rights of those who are one's special responsibility—might seem to be a genuine duty only for persons in offices and roles that are directly responsible for ensuring the ability of individuals (or a specific population) to fulfill their human rights, it actually applies to everyone who is responsible for anyone else in a matter related to their human rights. For instance, in addition to my obligations to persons in war-ravaged countries, I also have relevant connections to and obligations toward my children and other members of my family, as well as persons in my local community, my workplace, and my nation. My connections with most of these persons in matters related to their human rights will probably be very indirect, but so are most if not all of our connections to persons in the so-called Third World. In any event, these are connections to persons I am responsible for in some way. Therefore, insofar as these persons may also have meaningful and true human-rights-claims toward me, these claims are rightly incorporated into my deliberations about which of the various opportunities I have for responding to other persons' human rights should take priority.

In addition and at a minimum, when we recognize that our efforts to aid or to change systems that violate people's human rights, etc., cannot be responsive to all who have meaningful and true human-rights-claims on us, we would be intellectually dishonest to pretend that what is lost to those whom we cannot help under the circumstances is somehow less important than what we are able to do for those whom we do help in some way. If their human-rights-claims are meaningful and true, then they are all equally related to us as persons who legitimately address us with their claims.

While the emphasis in Shue's wording of Duty #1 is on refraining from depriving, it seems clear that Duty #1 also has implications for how we are required to act, at least in one important respect. We are obligated to relate to every other person in such a way as to affirm rather than deny his or her capacity to make claims on us regarding human rights—or better, to affirm our fundamental relationship as equals in very important ways.

Finally, it is worth noting that this implication of human-rights-claims correlates closely with Feinberg's suggestion at the end of his description of what is distinctive about rights-claims that "what is called 'human dignity' may simply be the recognizable capacity to assert claims."[30] After all, human dignity is one of the most frequent descriptions of what we affirm when we respond to others in matters of human rights. In other words, although Feinberg's proposed answer to the meaning-question about human rights led him to conclude that most human-rights-claims lacked a sufficiently definite *who* to be considered meaningful rights-claims, his understanding of the relationship of equals that is implied in every human-rights-claim suggests at least an openness on his part to the present proposal, namely that the *who* in a meaningful human-rights-claim is in fact the *Rest of Us*—that is, all of us.[31]

Conclusion

In this essay I have tried to show that we humans are all interconnected, related to one another as equals by a moral relationship in which each of us may legitimately claim of the others that they have obligations to respond when the human rights of any of us are violated or seriously at risk. This does not mean that all human-rights-claims are true or valid, nor does it mean that we must respond to every human-rights-claim we learn of. However, it does mean that every human-rights-claim is addressed to every one of us, and that we have an obligation to attend to such claims. In each case we must determine what the claim means for us by carefully considering what actions it implies for us, and to make a careful judgment about whether we are indeed obligated to act accordingly. These are important responsibilities, and we have them, each of us, to every one of us.

Notes

1. For the *United Nations' Universal Declaration of Human Rights* (1948), see http://www.un.org/en/documents/udhr/index.shtml (accessed July 29, 2014).
2. Joel Feinberg, "The Nature and Value of Rights," *Journal of Value Inquiry* 4 (1970), 243-57, reprinted in *Rights*, ed. David Lyons (Belmont, CA: Wadsworth, 1979), 78-91. All page references to this essay are to Lyons's edition. On Feinberg's view of rights and rights-claims, see also Feinberg, *Social Philosophy* (Englewood Cliffs NJ: Prentice-Hall, 1973), especially chapter 4.
3. Feinberg, "The Nature and Value of Rights," 89 (italics in the original).
4. Ibid.
5. Ibid., 89-90.
6. Onora O'Neill, *The Bounds of Justice* (Cambridge: Cambridge University Press, 2000), 99-11, 125, 132.
7. James Griffin, *On Human Rights* (Oxford, Oxford University Press, 2008), 209.

8. See H.L.A. Hart, "Definition and Theory in Jurisprudence," in *Essays in Jurisprudence and Philosophy* (Oxford, Clarendon Press, 1953), 21.

9. Gregory Vlastos, "Justice and Equality," in *Social Justice,* ed. Richard Brandt (Englewood Cliffs, NJ:Prentice-Hall, 1962), 31-72.

10. See Ronald Dworkin, *Taking Rights Seriously* (Cambridge, MA: Harvard University Press, 1977), xi, where the image of rights as trumps is introduced, as well as xi-xiv and 188-191, where Dworkin offers his description of the priority that rights-claims have over other moral considerations. See Griffin, *On Human Rights*, 20-22, for a critique of Dworkin's description.

11. In light of the difference between the meaning-conditions of rights-claims and the two kinds of truth-conditions of rights-claims—namely those dependent on the existence of some accepted social system (in the case of conventional- rights-claims) and those that are independent of any and all social systems (in the case of human-rights-claims)—we should note that even if this essay succeeds in showing that many human-rights-claims that Feinberg would classify as "manifesto rights" are indeed meaningful and therefore genuine rights-claims, it would still be necessary to show that they are true. However, it would be beyond the scope of this essay to pursue further the question of what makes rights-claims true or false.

12. Hart, *Definition and Theory in Jurisprudence,* 9.

13. The expression "fairly distinct" is needed here because there are likely to be some "untidy" rights-claims that cannot be put into one of these categories rather than the other. See H.L.A. Hart on the "open texture" of concepts in his *The Concept of Law* (Oxford: Oxford University Press, 1961), 124-32.

14. See Feinberg, "The Nature and Value of Rights," 84-85.

15. Griffin, *On Human Rights,* 110.

16. A similar argument is found in Chapter Two of Henry Shue, *Basic Rights,* 2nd ed. (Princeton University Press, 1996), although Shue's argument is specifically aimed at a different issue. Here he is seeking to undermine the proposal that there are meaningful human-rights-claims that require refraining, but no acting.

17. Griffin, *On Human Rights,* 110.

18. See the four requirements given earlier in this essay.

19. Moreover, Joy Gordon argues that attributing structural priority, which she calls "normative absoluteness," to human-rights-claims actually suppresses moral discourse rather than resolving it. See Joy Gordon, "The Concept of Human Rights: The History and Meaning of Its Politicization," *Brooklyn Journal of International Law* 23, no. 3 (1998): 689-791.

20. Feinberg, "The Nature and Value of Rights," 84, 87.

21. On the notion of "exhibiting a pattern of acceptance of whatever norms of behavior," see H.L.A. Hart, *The Concept of Law,* 54-55, and David Ozar, "Social Rules and Patterns of Behavior," *Philosophy Research Archives* 3 (1977), 1-15.

22. The question can be asked whether rights-talk about matters having little moral significance fails to be meaningful as a rights-claim because it lacks the requisite of moral priority. However, that question is beyond the scope of this essay.

23. See for example the discussion of informal relationships within hierarchical corporations in Kathryn Real King, *Corporations as Group Agents: Responsible Collectives in Theory and in Practice,* Doctoral Dissertation, Loyola University Chicago, 2010.

24. Shue's category of "basic rights" refers to and includes all of the material and social preconditions of a person's being able to exercise any other right. Although his wording is different, his focus is on the same kinds of

human-rights-claims that have been the focus of this essay, and he clearly supports the view that the *who* of meaningful human-rights-claims is the Rest of Us, which is to say all of us.

25. See Shue, *Basic Rights*, 60. For the sake of clarity, the word "violate" is used here in each instance in which Shue himself uses the word "deprive," i.e., as shorthand for "deprive the party making the human-rights-claim of the fulfillment of their basic rights."

26. Since rights-claims can be meaningful but false, as was explained earlier, the question of whether a particular rights-claim is true is always the next appropriate step after determining that the rights-claim is meaningful. Moreover, since the meaningfulness of most rights-claims is obvious, it is testing their truth that we are most often doing. Whether a human-rights-claim is true or not—i.e., whether it does in fact indicate a genuine obligation to act or refrain in some way on the part of the Rest of Us—depends (to oversimplify a very complex matter) on whether what it concerns is of sufficient moral importance in the life of the claimant. The philosophical and political theory literature on this issue is voluminous.

27. In this connection, however, and contrary to the position being criticized in this essay, when questions such as these cannot be resolved with certainty, it seems implausible to claim that the resulting indeterminacy of the *how* indicates that the conflicting human-rights-claims are therefore not meaningful.

28. Shue, *Basic Rights*, 18-19.

29. Shue, *Basic Rights*, 115.

30. Feinberg, "The Nature and Value of Rights," 87.

31. In a similar way, O'Neill clearly supports the equality of all humans and, by implication, a relationship of all humans such that each of us has obligations to respond to the most morally significant unfulfilled needs of other

persons. However, her discussion of rights-claims is uncompromising on the requirement that the *who* of a rights-claim must be determinate, and therefore her claim can be distinguished from the openness identified here in Feinberg's views. This openness is articulated in his willingness, cited above, to forgive manifesto writers "when they speak of [such claims] as if they are already actual rights" and his saying, "I accept the moral principle that to have an unfulfilled need is to have a kind of claim against the world, even if against no one in particular." See O'Neill, *Bounds of Justice,* 89.

5

The Birth of Rights Talk

Thomas E. Wren

In the following pages I offer an extended "case study" of the way discourse shapes moral thought and vice-versa. It is a rather unusual study since the case under investigation is the long historical transformation of a philosophical concept, including the language that houses it. Just how did the modern discourse of *subjective rights* develop from the earlier, very different moral discourses centered on *objective rightness?* The discourses of the ancient Greeks and Romans were quite different from our own discourse of moral and legal rights, such as the right to vote or own property, not to mention current discussions of controversial human rights issues such as whether rulings about rights violations should apply to everyone regardless of his or her culture or background. Scholarly opinions vary regarding the historical origins of our contemporary rights talk, but I will follow the lead of a handful of philosophically savvy classicists and medievalists who in the late

20th century reopened the discussion of the historical origins of rights talk. I will try to show why that discourse did not begin until the Middle Ages, was initially focused on a small set of urgent issues such as property ownership and political authority, and had philosophical foundations that went far beyond the Aristotelian notion of "natural law" that was so important for Thomas Aquinas and other medieval philosophers and theologians.

I will begin with the early Greeks' idea of objective rightness as the "correct" way to act (i.e., to do the right thing, to follow the path of righteousness, and so on). Then I will take up the underlying philosophical conception of rightness in the Romans' long and slowly evolving legal tradition. I will finish with a defense of an important though controversial claim about the seldom recognized medieval origins of our current notion of personal rights as moral demands that individuals can press against other individuals or even against society at large. Until recently (about thirty years ago), the consensus among philosophers as well as historians, classists, and legal scholars was that our familiar notion of personal rights did not enter Western discourse until the 17th century, or at most just a few decades earlier. However, over the last decades a small but growing number of intellectual historians have disagreed, arguing that in the high Middle Ages there suddenly emerged a radically different, plainly subjective conception of rights as moral powers that people simply *have*. These powers were thought to include the personal rights that every individual has to own property and to be treated in certain ways, or more generally, *to be respected.*

I regard this emergence as a transformation rather than an evolution of moral discourse for three perhaps obvious but nonetheless important reasons. The first is that what changed was human language, not the impersonal genetic properties that are the subject of evolutionary paradigms. The second reason is that language, unlike biological processes, is inherently self-referential and self-correcting. ("Is this the right word?" "Do I need to say more?" "Let's put it this way!" etc.) The third reason is that the changes in question should not be understood as analogues of what probability theorists variously call "Brownian Movements," "Random Walks," or, more picturesquely, "Drunken Strolls" from one self-contained way of life or worldview to another. On the contrary, the changes are parts of an intentional, largely self-directed process in which groups of human beings are simultaneously agents of change and the products of those changes. In other words, in the domain of normative discourse as in other domains of human intentionality such as aesthetic sensibility or ego development, human collectives have created their own languages and intellectual histories just as they have created their own cultural, political, and technological histories. They have done so knowingly, since language inherited from the past provides part of the context within which new language is developed. In short, the context within which rights talk takes place is a mix of social forces, personal talents and passions, and of course economic structures.

In this respect the development of the notion of rights resembles the pattern of collective agency described by the social movement theorist Alberto Merlucci:

> Individuals acting collectively *construct* their action by defining in cognitive terms these possibilities and limits, while at the same time interacting with others in order to "organize" (i.e., to make sense of) their common behavior. Collective action is not a unitary empirical phenomenon. Whatever unity exists should be considered

the result and not the starting point, a fact to be explained rather than assumed. When actors produce their collective action they define both themselves and their environment (other actors, available resources, opportunities and obstacles).[1]

However, most of the individuals in the narrative that follows did not see themselves as *agents of change* (Merlucci's own model) but rather as *conservators of old values during times of change,* such as when the Roman Republic took shape in the fifth century BC, again during the breakdown and aftermath of the Roman Empire, and finally during the reformulation of property ownership *(dominium)* and other forms of self-determination that took place in the so-called "feudal" order of the 12th century. Ironically, it was their very conservatism that shaped the changes that took place during those years.

There are many ways to tell the story of moral and legal rights, but in what follows I will track—or at least point out—certain large-scale changes in social structure (including some of its political dimensions and with special attention to changes in the concept of property) and in the corresponding patterns of discourse (especially philosophical and legal exchanges) that both produced and resulted from the legal systems that determined privileges and duties. The first of these (changes in social structure) includes the transitions from the Greek city-states to the Roman Monarchy, Republic, and Empire, as well as the early and middle centuries of the feudal era. The second (changes in patterns of discourse) includes Socratic dialogues, the lectures and conversations of Stoics and other philosophers, the Roman jurists' textbooks, official legal rescripts, the early Church's patristic writings and sermons, medieval glosses, ecclesiastical rulings, theological disputations, and (of special relevance here) discussions of the elusive notion of *property,* to name just a few of the many forms of discourse that generated Western conceptions of "right" over the two millennia under discussion. As we will see, those discourses shaped and were shaped by large-scale changes in social structures such as the rise and fall of the Roman Empire and the institutionalization of Christianity as a political force.

Of course each of these periods of ancient and medieval history has its own massive literature produced by brilliant and tenacious historians, philosophers, and other sorts of intellectuals. In what follows, I will focus on the events and structures that formed the matrix from which the concept of personal rights eventually emerged. As the political theorist and historian Ian Shapiro once said, "If we want to understand our own beliefs as fully and critically as possible, it is essential ... to see where our beliefs come from and what functions they serve in the contemporary world."[2] In other words, I will provide not only a short history of rights discourse but also an exhibit of the discursive foundations of social construction itself.

To sum up so far: it is generally understood by intellectual historians and scholars in normative disciplines such as philosophy and theology that before people talked of "rights" in the sense of personal claims or powers they talked of "rightness" in the sense of an objective standard, a proper order of things, or the correct way to behave. The transition from rightness to rights, be they natural rights, legal rights, divine rights, or—most recently—human rights, has been examined from many different perspectives but almost never from the perspective of discourse theory, using the latter term in a very wide sense.[3] In the following pages I will try to do just that, beginning with an account of the classical

Greek conception of *dike*, then discussing at greater length the Roman notions of *jus* and *dominium*, and finally reviewing the early medieval discussions of rights as powers or, better, as claims that individuals can make against other individuals or even against society at large.

How the latter, so-called subjective sense of the term "right" continued to develop after the Middle Ages, that is, in the Renaissance and early modernity (most famously, in the social contract theories of Thomas Hobbes and John Locke), is fairly well-known, and so I will not discuss those thinkers here. Nor will I discuss the so-called "high" and "late" medieval thinkers such as William of Ockham who are sometimes treated as the transition figures from the classical objective notion of rightness to the early modern subjective notion of rights as powers. It will be enough to show that by the early 1200's the subjective notion of rights was firmly in place even though it was still rather crude and by no means the dominant view among academic philosophers and theologians.

The "Rightness" Discourse of the Ancient Greeks

Although contemporary scholars disagree regarding exactly when rights talk started, the consensus is that there was no concept of moral rights until centuries after the ancient Greek and Roman eras. To be sure, there was an extensive and powerful moral discourse in those early times, but it had different conceptual foundations and was centered on objective normative concepts such as *rightness, the just order, straightness,* and simply *the way things should be.* For our purposes, the most relevant of the ancient terms are the Greek *dikaion,* its root *dike,* and later the Latin *jus* and its plural *jura,* all of which have been translated as "justice," "law," or sometimes "what is right."[4] Unfortunately, some translations are misleading since they present these terms as meaning a personal virtue, in the same genus as prudence, temperance, or fortitude. Among classicists and philologists, however, there is general agreement[5] that in ancient Greece and Rome these words always referred to objective states of affairs in which social relationships, personal dispositions, and even the physical and moral structures of the universe are rightly ordered, balanced, or otherwise "in sync." For instance, in his *Works and Days,* the early Greek poet Hesiod exhorted unjust rulers who "twist the courses of justice aslant" to "straighten" their decisions, and he praised those "who give straight judgments to strangers and to the men of the land, and go not aside from what is just."[6] In his *Republic*, Plato identified justice as a balance of reason and appetites even as he cited Pindar's use of the term to designate the quality of men who "avoid the crooked ways of deceit," and of course the tragic flaw of Sophocles' Oedipus was his blindness to the demands of *dike*.[7]

But what about the equally ancient concept of duty, which is often understood as the reciprocal of the concept of rights? Surely, one might say, where there were duties there must have been rights. However, this is too quick. Granted, the idea of "duty" (*deon* in Greek, *debitum* or *officium* in Latin) is an equally venerable concept. Even so, in ancient moral discourse the idea of duty was correlated not with rights but rather with the concept of justice, understood as the objectively right order or natural law. That correlation is quite different from the modern correlation of rights and duties, in which both terms are understood in a subjective sense as something a person *has*. The difference between the ancient and modern views is easily seen if we consider ordinary non-moral types of rightness and dutifulness such as the right way to row a boat. Every oarsman knows that there are objectively right and wrong ways for an individual to row, as well as for a crew to row as a team. In all social interactions—including the interactions between captains and their crews—there are settled expectations that can be expressed in the language of duties or "oughts," even though the normative character of these expectations is usually more pragmatic than moral. In short, to get the vessel moving, the crew "ought" to work in the "right" way.

There is no doubt that the ancient Greeks and Romans had a fine-grained vocabulary for what we now call "duties" and "obligations," but that does not mean that their sense of objective rightness corresponds to our own subjective notion of rights. For them, duties were obligations to do the right thing, not demands to honor the rights of other people. This ancient way of understanding rights and duties still shows up in modern discourse. Boy Scouts promise to be "morally straight," Catholics say at the beginning of the canon of the mass that it is "right and just" to give thanks to God,[8] and a sympathetic traffic policeman might tell an elderly driver that "by right" or "rightly" he should write a traffic ticket but instead will simply "do the right thing" and only issue a warning.

Admittedly, it can be hard to see a difference between the ancient Greeks' *deon* and our modern notions of duty and obligation. Scholars are divided on this issue. For instance, the highly respected natural law theorist Fred Miller has argued that Thomas Aquinas and other medieval scholars had read Aristotle as having a subjective sense of rights and duties, and that they were correct to do so. Not surprisingly, Miller has been severely criticized as having twisted the meanings of those two terms (i.e., *deon* and *dike*) from their original context of worth and desert in order to fit them into a modern context of rights and duties.[9] My own view on the matter is less harsh, and can be summarized as follows. The ancient Greeks, as represented in the poetry of Hesiod and Homer and the tragedies of Aeschylus, Sophocles, and Euripides, seem to have understood the mindset of "justice" as a general respect for the transcendent order of the universe (including its moral realm as well as the physical cosmos) and, by extension, for the divine beings who preside over that order. If so, then it would not be surprising to discover similar attitudes in the centuries that followed.

Hellenist Transition: The Stoics and Property Rights *(Dominium)*

The Greeks' conception of rightness as an objective reality was fully assimilated by the Romans in spite of major differences in their other philosophical outlooks and in their social-political structures. To see how this played out, it will be useful first to take a brief look at the transition from Greek to Roman dominance in philosophical thought, as well as in the worldly domains of commerce and military power. The nearly three-century transition period (323-30 BC)[10] that is now called "the Hellenic Age" was remarkably short compared to the respective lengths of the classical Greek and Roman eras. Indeed, it is easy to forget that the Roman era lasted over a thousand years, much longer than the archaic and classical periods of ancient Greece and even a bit longer than the thousand years between the High Middle Ages and our own day.

To be sure, there was considerable overlap (roughly two and a half centuries) of the Hellenic Age and Rome's Monarchy and early Republic. During that time, small self-standing Greek city states reminiscent of fifth-century Athens thrived and then declined, partly for financial reasons (more bluntly: the Romans had conquered and looted them) and partly because Rome was rapidly replacing Greece as the military and commercial center of the Mediterranean world. The days of grand metaphysical systems were also over, and the most prominent intellectuals of the region—for our purposes also the most relevant—were the Stoics, for whom philosophical discourse was essentially a "therapy of desire."[11] An important part of that therapy was the analysis and transformation of existing theories of natural law (especially Aristotle's) and with it their conceptions of property and ownership or "dominion," which anticipated the discourse of rights and duties that would emerge in the High Middle Ages.

Some of those early Stoics were Greeks, others Romans, and a few neither, but most of what we know of their specifically ethical teachings comes from later Roman commentaries such as Diogenes Laertius' *Lives of Eminent Philosophers* in the third century AD. By the end of the Republic, most of the typical Roman citizen's knowledge of the early Stoics' teachings about justice, the natural law, and cosmopolitan ideals had been provided by the remarkable first century BC figure Marcus Tullius Cicero (106-43 BC), who though not a Stoic himself was deeply influenced by their moral teachings.[12] Cicero was a force in his own right: a brilliant lawyer and orator, an eloquent if not especially original philosopher, and a prodigious commentator on Rome's history and its social and legal structures. He parlayed the Stoics' notion of world citizenship into a powerful demythologized conception of justice and incorporated their notion of property into his own writings on the nature of law. As a legal advocate, he was fully aware of the complexities of Roman law, and although not born in Rome, he cherished, as did every upper-class citizen, Rome's tradition of order and organization. This tradition—passion might be a better word—would be celebrated a generation later in Vergil's *Aeneid*,[13] which provided

Romans with a mirror in which to admire themselves. "For you, O Romans," Vergil wrote, "these are your skills, to establish law and order within a framework of peace."

However, many of these skills had pre-Roman roots, such as the early Stoics' quite remarkable discussions of property. That conversation began in the late fourth or early third century BC in an ongoing, face-to-face exchange between two of the early heads of their Academy mentioned above, namely Zeno and Chrysippus. In their conversations with each other and with their students, they forged a distinctive concept of private ownership that was itself based on the longstanding Greek notion of natural law. This law was *descriptive* in the same way that scientific formulas like the law of gravity describe features of the physical universe and *prescriptive* in the way that other normative systems such as the Decalogue and the Tao prescribe principles of the moral universe.

The early Stoics did not hesitate to use vivid metaphors such as primal fire and personalized deities to portray their concept of a cosmic order *(logos),* and one of their earliest metaphors was that of a cosmic city populated by divine as well as human citizens. Unlike the biblical Garden of Eden, their city was understood as a heuristic device rather than as a historical fact. This difference was reflected in the medieval debates over whether there was personal property (i.e., dominion) before the Fall or only a purely communal system.[14] However, there was no such debate among the Stoics or their Roman successors, all of whom (except for the early Roman Christians) believed that the human members of the ideal city were property owners by their very nature as self-conscious agents and embodied selves. (Presumably the gods who also lived in the Stoics' city had no need of property.)

Few details of this foundational myth have survived, but it shaped the thoughts and discourse of the later Stoics and Roman intellectuals such as Cicero and the early Seneca, as well as the conversations of ordinary Roman citizens, most of whom simply assumed that the firmly established institution of private property was a natural fact. But what led the early Stoics to create this little story?

In my view, the best answer to this question is that for them a sense of proprietorship was an intrinsic structure of human consciousness. Later in this chapter I will claim that the modern concept of subjective rights, especially property rights, can be traced back to the 12th century canonists. However, their Christianized notion of dominion was foreshadowed by ideas of the early Stoics and undoubtedly influenced by the heavy use that Cicero made of it in his *De Officiis*.[15] As the classics scholar and philosopher A. A. Long has shown,[16] the Stoics' view of property was based on the joint premises that (1) every human individual is the rightful owner of his or her own person and (2) our relations with other humans are shaped by our natural tendency to interact with them as fellow property owners.

In other words, part of the deep structure of property discourse is that each interlocutor deploys a first-person conception of self-ownership in second- and third-person discourse, and thereby constructs a primitive but distinctive conception of private property as a feature of his or her personal identity. If so, then the point of the Stoics' story of a cosmic city is that ownership of one's self is a necessary condition of being a person and that the mutual recognition of this principle is a necessary condition of living in society. For Chrysippus and later for Cicero, a corollary of this principle was the notion of fair play: "A runner on the racetrack must strain and compete with all his might to come first," wrote

Chrysippus, "but on no account may he trip or shove a fellow competitor; and likewise in life, there is nothing wrong with an individual's seeking what is in his own interest, but it is unjust to deprive another."[17]

The Roman Monarchy and the *Mos Majorum*

One of the most striking features of the nearly two and a half centuries of Roman monarchy (753-509 BC) is the absence of any codified or written legal system. Like the Greek historian Herodotus (485-430 BC), the Romans of that period believed that custom was king. The so-called *mos majorum* ("the way of the ancestors") determined the norms, models, and status patterns of their society, which is to say the shape of its private, political, and military dimensions. Of these, the first two are most relevant here. At the center of the private dimension was the family, over which the *paterfamilias* had absolute power but was expected to act responsibly (which is to say in accordance with traditions), if only to avoid censure from the wider community. The political structures were also completely shaped and mandated by tradition rather than by written statues. Once a king was on the throne, he had carte blanche, except that he could not wage war without the consent of the Senate that had elected him.

This practice worked fairly well until the reign of the infamous Tarquinius Superbus, who, to put it mildly, left much to be desired. (When he was assassinated in 509 BC the monarchy came to an end.) However, many of the monarchs were honorable and successful leaders. Auguries were read, sacrifices made to the gods, and the Romans were generally successful in their military campaigns against their Etruscan, Sabinian, and Latin neighbors. Rome's size and power grew rapidly, and with this growth came greater and wider patterns of property ownership or dominion, acquired through either conquest, the cultivation of open land, or ordinary buying and selling.

Of particular interest here is the way private property was bought and sold. The buyer and seller—both of whom had to be Romans—met in front of witnesses and engaged in a short ritual that consummated the sale. The sale itself was always understood as a private transaction or *actio* between two parties; however, it was carried out in public in order to ensure agreement on all sides. The transfer of "immovable property" *(res mancipi)* was symbolized by striking a scale with a copper ingot, at which point ownership was recognized by everyone as having been transferred from seller to buyer. For the sake of good order this public ceremony was required for the transfer of properties associated with agriculture, including land, houses, slaves, and farm animals, but it was not required for common objects, for which simple delivery sufficed as an unspoken transfer of title. In either case, though, what is important for our purposes is that although legal procedures were involved, the *actio* itself was a private arrangement between two parties, not (that is, not until later in the Empire) a new relationship created by the state. In short, the representative of the state was only a special sort of witness to the exchange, in roughly the same way that a contemporary minister or justice of the peace will declare to the community after the exchange of wedding vows that the two participants have just made a marriage contract.

It is sometimes suggested that Roman law during the monarchy consisted entirely of folk customs and traditions, but this is not quite correct. There were also formal decrees, issued on an ad hoc basis by kings or by the Senate during the intervals between kings. For instance, at a certain point an exception was made to the standing assumption that only the paterfamilias could own property, which allowed sons who went to war to keep for themselves whatever property they seized in battle. Even so, unwritten custom plus occasional edicts do not add up to a legal system, and so it is quite correct to consider the famous Twelve Tables of the new Republic as the true starting point of the Roman legal system as well as the first technical use of the term *jus*.

The Early Roman Republic

After Tarquinus, the monarchy was replaced by the early Republic (509-250 BC), which had its own coming of age problems, especially during its first six decades. Of these pains, the most important was the social struggle between the patricians, who could trace their ancestry back to the first hundred members of the king's advisory council, and the plebeians, who were less distinguished but nonetheless longstanding Roman citizens. After a period of discontent (during which the plebeian work force used the threat of secession to secure concessions from the ruling patricians), the first ten Tables of the Law were published in 450 BC.[18] It was the result of what seems to have been the first case of formal cross-class political discourse, which Livy described as follows:

> Each citizen was to consider each point privately, then in discourse with his friends, and then in public discussion.... Afterwards, the laws were voted on and passed at the assembly, in voting by centuries [blocs of income groups] which, even to this time, has been the source of all public and private jurisprudence.[19]

Contemporary legal historians agree with Livy. They regard the famous Twelve Tables of the new Republic as the true starting point of the Roman legal system as well as the first technical use of the term *jus*. The word appears in three of the twelve tables, and the last occurrence is directly relevant to property law. (The Latin text is *uti lingua nuncupassit, ita jus esto,* which can be translated as "When a formal declaration has been made [of, say, a bond for the conveyance of property], then it is a *jus*," which is to say: then it is legally binding.)

It is important to recognize the structural significance of this new legal discourse. With the greater social and economic complexity of the young Republic came new legal issues and new procedures in *criminal law* (since crimes were now offenses against the *res publica,* not against the *rex* himself), in foreigner or *peregrine law* (since with Rome's new dominance of the Mediterranean came increasingly complex issues involving foreigners), but most of all with *civil law* (especially with contract and property disputes).

Even so, several of the old suppositions about the nature of ownership remained intact. As in the monarchy, property was understood as pre-legal dominion: as something that an individual (or family) had as a result of conquest, cultivation, exchange, inheritance, or in some cases simple discovery. It was pre-legal in the sense that transfers of ownership were private arrangements or "deals" made between individuals, and the function of the state was simply to record the facts of ownership, including the fact that a transfer of ownership had taken place.

However, property claims became more complicated after the monarchy: there were more people, more properties, and more complicated exchanges. There were also new political structures, from which new legal procedures quickly developed. The king was replaced by two consuls, each of whom held office for a single year and, in addition to their other duties, presided over criminal trials. Non-criminal trials, including those involving property issues, were adjudicated by ordinary citizens of good reputation. However, to help these citizen-judges try a case, the head magistrate or "praetor" would prepare a checklist or "formulary" that set forth the questions that needed to be answered before a verdict could be rendered. This arrangement was agreeable to all concerned for two reasons that reflected the democratic ethos of the Republic: the first stage of the process (determining the salient categories and legal terms for the case at hand) was handled by an impartial and highly placed political authority, and the second stage (the actual determination of what happened) was handled by a person who had already been accepted by the litigants themselves. In this respect civil trials were more like today's private arbitration hearings than public courtroom trials: the contending parties agreed in advance to accept the arbitrator's decision, there was no question of appeal, and the judge/arbitrator could ask his own questions about the facts of the case and, when necessary, demand to see documents or to hear witnesses not provided by either of the parties involved.

The Later Republic

By about 250 BC (halfway through the republican era), things became quite different than they had been immediately after the monarchy. By then, Rome dominated the western part of the Mediterranean area, it was increasingly wealthy and populous, and many of the old customs and practices were withering away. One of these practices was the praetor's having to draw up the formularies for civil trials. To what must have been the great relief of everyone, that task was delegated to competent private individuals. These were the jurists, who at first were simply well-educated laymen but later were highly skilled professional legal scholars. It was they who set the ground rules for civil cases, for instance by distinguishing essential issues from aggravating or mitigating circumstances.

With this and other changes the process became even more like contemporary arbitrations hearings than lawsuits. For instance, one of the tasks assigned to the consulting jurist was to show the judge how to repair the breach between the two parties. Another even more important difference was the new practice by the praetors and their jurist advisors of specifying the remedies that would correct any injustices that might come to light in the course of the trial, such as the finding that a defendant did in fact owe money to the plaintiff or—of special relevance to our inquiry—that the defendant was occupying or otherwise holding or using the plaintiff's property against the latter's will. Theoretically, drawing up a rescript that called for a transfer of property would be the equivalent of establishing a new law, which was beyond a praetor's power, and so an ingenious workaround was used. Since neither the judge, the jurist, nor the praetor had the power to replace the legal owner of the property in question, the unfortunate non-owner was awarded physical control of the property with the stipulation that the arrangement would last until enough years had gone by for the property to be considered legally his.

This treatment of physical possession as de facto possession but not de jure ownership would eventually erode the very concept of personal dominion, but in the later Republic it was regarded as a fair resolution of inherently unjust situations. To twenty-first century readers, all this may seem very strange, but it makes sense once we understand what was actually going on in cases involving property. As already noted, in the Republic an owner did not hold title to his property *because* the legal system granted it, but rather the other way around: the court merely *recognized* the fact that in the normal case the person who possessed a piece of property was its owner—a fact that was usually obvious but sometimes had to be sorted out or tweaked in legal hearings. In short, the state formally recognized ownership in order to ensure smooth business transactions, but the owner-ship itself was understood as a pre-existing reality.

The Classical Period of the Empire

All of this changed in the classical period of the Empire (27 BC-284 AD), when the judges in civil disputes were more focused on possible damages to the political system (which is to say, to the Emperor's authority) than on the issues between the litigants themselves. However, the change was gradual, since Augustus and the other early emperors always tried to represent themselves not as dictators or kings but as "the first among equals" or *primus inter pares*. Also, by the end of the Republic, disputation had become a high art: legal scholarship as well as courtroom forensics was very sophisticated, with important differences among the jurists themselves.

The first three centuries of the Empire, usually called the Principate, made up what is now probably the best-known period of Roman history, if only because of the huge number of popular novels and films set in that period.[20] The Principate began when the Roman senate gave Octavian the titles of *Augustus* and *Princeps* in 27 BC, and lasted until 284 AD,[21] which as we will see was the beginning of Diocletian's reign and the Dominate period. The juristic discourse of the early Principate quickly became more sophisticated and comprehensive than it had ever been during the Republic. It was as though sometime toward the middle of the first century, the legal world reached a critical mass and then exploded into volumes of philosophical speculation, textbooks for law students, and court archives of previous cases.

The Romans were still getting used to the idea of an absolute ruler directing an imperial court when two rival groups of jurists emerged, the Proculians and the Sabinians,[22] who had what might be called contrasting epistemologies of jurisprudence. They debated whether juridical decisions should be based entirely on precedents (the Proculians) or also on external norms of rationality such as philosophy, dialectics, grammatology (philology), and history (the Sabinians). As it turned out, the two approaches usually called for the same verdict in the case at hand, although for different reasons. Thanks especially to this short-lived debate, juristic discourse in the Principate sharpened, expanded, and became very sophisticated. However, by the second century, the contest between the two groups was over, not because either side won but rather because their differences no longer seemed relevant in Rome's increasingly top-down political environment. Apparently the jurists of the later Principate were no more inclined to meta-level speculation than most of our lawyers are today.

A second, more fundamental development in Roman law during the early Empire was the new status of the jurists themselves. Although some continued to work as self-employed consultants and others took in students or served as advisors to private individuals, most became salaried members of the empirical court. In this capacity they wrote formularies as before, but now with an eye toward consistency with the policies of the Emperor. Some had the duty to collect and, where appropriate, comment on the rescripts and other writings of earlier jurists such as the prolific Domitus Ulpian

(c. 170-228), and others wrote simply because they liked to write. A few of these author-jurists stand out, not only because of their prominence in their own day but also because (as we will see) three centuries later much of their work was preserved in the famous *Digest* of the Eastern Emperor Justinian the Great (527-565).[23]

The third development was the most important of all, though little noticed at the time. It began during the Emperor Hadrian's reign (117-138), when he rewarded his retiring soldiers by granting them dominion over local estates in newly conquered territories. However, with his gift came the qualification that if they later decided to live elsewhere, ownership would revert back to the Emperor. In other words, what his soldiers received was a very provisional sort of dominion, which strictly speaking is a contradiction in terms. In subsequent centuries, other anomalies surfaced in the absence of carefully wrought and recorded juridical decisions. To my knowledge, this is the first recorded instance of an emperor's claiming to be the personal owner of conquered territories, but there is no reason to think that it was the first time an emperor had declared himself a privileged property owner.

In itself there was nothing illogical about the idea of an emperor owning such territories since, as I have already noted, from the earliest days of the monarchy one of the ways that property could be acquired was by conquest. However, it was somewhat of a stretch to use the word *dominium* to describe what the soldiers were to receive, since a provisional *dominium* would seem to be a contradiction in terms. In subsequent centuries, other such anomalies appeared as the quality of judicial reasoning declined. As we will see, as time went on, the concept of *dominium* evolved from an undisputed, primitive given to a rather strange amalgam of de facto possession, imperial power, and juridical confusion.[24]

The Dominate

The Dominate (284-476) was not a happy period of Roman history. It inspired relatively little great art or literature (except for some elegant churches and religious literature produced after Constantine's conversion to Christianity in 312), and there were no grand military conquests of rich new territories. However, for our story this era was the most relevant time of Rome's entire legal history. From the period's basic social, political, and (most important of all) economic structures came a new system of civil law so dysfunctional that was only a matter of time (albeit, a very long time) before it would collapse from its own weight and be replaced, slowly but surely, by a system based on the novel idea that individuals have personal, subjective rights. However, before we consider that later development, we should recognize the difference between the relatively smooth legal procedures of the Principate and those that developed very early in the Dominate and lasted more or less unchanged until well after the end of the empire.

At the beginning of the Dominate, which is to say at the start of Diocletian's reign (284-305), the Romans' civil court procedures and the decisions they produced were no longer shaped by seasoned jurists and established customs but rather by poorly trained judges who reported directly to the Emperor. The jurists themselves were little more than clerks for the judges rather than the other way around, as in the Republic.[25] Since there was no longer a pre-established checklist (the old formulary) drawn up by an external legal expert, the judge could shape his verdict in terms of whatever criteria seemed relevant, including written documents and considerations about degrees of culpability, such as whether there had been malice aforethought.

Unlike earlier civil proceedings, in the Dominate a judge's verdict was not always final, even when he himself had gathered most or all of the evidence. Either party could appeal his decision, sometimes all the way to the Emperor, even though the appellate procedures were very complex and unpredictable. In the case of property disputes, the winner no longer had to recover compensation from the loser for whatever damages he had sustained, but could simply ask the court to do so for him. In short, the old function of civil law as a device to help individuals resolve differences between themselves was replaced by the one that many, perhaps most, nations have today, in which the state is entirely responsible for investigating, adjudicating, and resolving the entire issue.

For instance, at the end of a trial about property the Emperor or the judges who acted in his name *awarded* legal control of the property (which at some deep level still belonged to the Emperor) to one of the contestants, unlike the judges in earlier times who simply *recorded* the jury's decision as to who had the better claim to be the true, pre-legal owner. It was, therefore, quite logical for Diocletian to give himself the title of *Dominus*, since the entire empire was now his personal property or dominion. This statement of imperial ownership had been foreshadowed two centuries earlier by Hadrian's above-mentioned gift of colonial land to his retired soldiers, but it was only in the aptly named Dominate that the Emperor's universal ownership was formally proclaimed. Like Hadrian's gift, the property that any citizen held during the Dominate was at most a very provisional sort of dominion. In sum, the court decided property disputes in the name of the Emperor because, after all, he was the *real* owner.

But how did all this come about? What were the relevant large-scale structural differences between the earlier and later periods of the Empire? The answer to these questions is really quite simple: after decades of mismanagement and internal strife (much of it bloody), the Empire was broke. No new wealthy territories had been conquered, domestic production of grain and other goods had declined because of droughts and social unrest, nearly every non-Roman living in Rome and the colonies had been granted citizenship, and Rome's local population was increasingly foreign-born and landless. Whatever else one might say about Diocletian's first years as Emperor, they were definitely decisive. He ruled with an iron fist, replaced the title *Princeps* with that of *Dominus,* took direct control of the treasury and legal system, and after just a few years, divided the Empire into four more or less separate regions, each governed by a junior emperor. To replenish the imperial treasury, Diocletian levied heavy taxes on the citizens, new and old, and was especially diligent in collecting from the wealthy landowners, regardless of whether they farmed their own land, rented it out, or just let it lie fallow. Under his reign a form of virtual slavery called the colonate emerged, which had its own rules for property management.[26] He also insisted that landholders increase their productivity, since along with other chronic problems of debt and military failures came a series of famines and droughts, two challenges that previous emperors had already learned to take very seriously. Not surprisingly, as the Emperor and his subjects struggled with these problems, the old notion of property as a pre-legal fact sank beneath the waves. In short, a side effect of the deep changes in the empire's social, economic, and political structures during the Dominate was that the law itself was no longer what it used to be, and neither were the lawyers' discursive skills.

An important part of the fallout from these structural changes as well as from the general decline in legal competence was a serious confusion in the distant lower courts (as well as in not-so-low regional courts) regarding the difference between simple *possession* (physical control) of a piece of property and *dominion* (ownership) over it. Usually a person who owns something also possesses it and vice versa, but holding title is much different than actually using or controlling a thing. Sometimes such a split is perfectly legal and acceptable to all concerned, as when a tenant farmer not only lives on an absentee landlord's property but also has the guaranteed "use of its fruits," which lawyers call the "usufruct" of the property. However, owners and tenants did not always agree on the terms of their arrangements, in which case they typically went to court.

During the Principate, the court process had been fairly simple. An owner who had been denied access to or possession of what he considered his property—or a tenant who believed that he actually held a valid title—could petition the court in one of two ways. The first way was for the owner to request what was called a *vindicatio*. In this case, success meant that the judge vindicated the property (in today's parlance, he "liberated it") from anyone who physically possessed it—typically, by actually living on the property and controlling what was done with it. The process was only a little different in the opposite case, when the petitioner was the current possessor. In that case, a judge who favored the tenant did not vindicate the property but instead granted an *interdict* that allowed the petitioner to resist any attempt by the owner to forcibly seize the disputed property. In other words, if there were a dispute, the only strategy available to a threatened owner was to try to secure a *vindicatio* (unless that alternative had already been attempted, since no appeals were allowed), and the only strategy available to an unhappy tenant (the possessor) was to request an *interdict*, which would require the owner to stop trying to take possession of the property. That was the way things had worked in the orderly classical law courts of the Principate. However, legal procedures were quite different in the unruly courts of the Dominate. There, the option of seeking a *vindicatio* was available to anyone who felt entitled to possess the thing, at which point the very distinction between ownership and possession became problematic.

Before the Dominate, Roman law had distinguished between a *contract* to dispose of property (by which I mean any sort of agreement to sell it) and the actual *transfer of ownership* from the seller to the buyer. The contract imposed duties on the seller to convey the property to the buyer and on the buyer to pay the agreed price, but it had no direct effect on the fact of ownership itself. Until the conveyance, the property remained the seller's; once delivered (but only then), it belonged to the buyer. However, in the Dominate that distinction also became blurred and the new rule was that "ownership is transferred by a sale," which is to say no separate conveyance was needed for the transfer of title. Commenting on this new formulation, the legal historian Peter Stein has made the following astute observation:

> To those who appreciate the precision and exact ways of thought characteristic of the classical period, such cases give post-classical law a sloppy, degenerate appearance. It is unscientific and they designate it "vulgar law," by analogy with the vulgar Latin of the period during which it was being transformed into the separate Romance languages. Others stress that law has to adapt itself to the conditions of the society to which it applies. If they demand more informality at the expense of technicality, that should be seen as a sign of legal vitality and "organic growth."[27]

To this, I would only add that regardless of which view one takes regarding the vulgarization of Roman law, the important thing is that what happened could very well *not* have happened. Discourse, even professional, rule-governed discourse, is inherently unpredictable and always open to new perspectives and unexpected forms of metonymy. In this respect, the Romans' new conception of ownership is like the invention of courtly love or the game of rugby: often novel and crude, but always something of a surprise and often full of promise.[28]

In the famous year 476 AD, the Western Empire collapsed. To borrow T.S. Eliot's famous line, it ended not with a bang but a whimper. By then, the great Roman legal system had nearly fizzled out. As the Empire ground to its halt, lack of legal talent was only one of several problems with the Roman legal system. Another was the increasing independence of the provincial law courts, where judges and jurists worked with little or no oversight from Rome. Still a third problem was what historians now call the "vulgarization" of Roman law, by which they mean the debasing influence of barbarian customs on the classical forms of Roman law and the Latin language, especially those identified with the early part of the Empire. Finally, we must add to all these considerations the harsh fact that in tumultuous times, property lines are often blurred or simply erased, and ownership becomes a matter of *de facto* possession rather than *de jure* entitlement. It seems safe to say that had it not been for the firmly established church,[29] the very institution of legal ownership could have withered away.

From Empire to Christendom

By 476, what was left of the Roman legal system would have been unrecognizable to the jurists and judges of the Republic and Principate. Poorly trained lawyers were only part of the difference. What historians now call the "vulgar law" of the provinces, where invading tribes had either imported their own legal traditions or forced crucial changes in the local applications of Roman law, also formed an important part of the new legal scene. A still greater force for change, though, was the influence of Christianity in every sector of daily life, including the legal sector. Even before the Western Empire ceased to exist, much of its authority had been replaced by the pastoral and administrative practices of the Roman church. Its rules shaped not only private conversations between its members but also the Christians' public discourse, which included discussions of the church's responsibilities to the sick and poor as well as sermons about the importance of obedience to the religious authorities. Roman life had always had a religious dimension, but never anything like Christianity's scripturally-based norms of charity, humility, and the worship of a carpenter's crucified son. One need not be a theologian to recognize the differences as well as similarities between the value systems of the republican and classical Romans such as Cicero and Ulpian, on the one hand, and those of the Christians of the late Dominate, such as Ambrose (c. 340-397) and Augustine (354-430), on the other.[30]

After the confusions and hardships of the three centuries following the fall of Rome, life became much easier thanks to the evolving social and political structures of the Carolingian and post-Carolingian periods.[31] However, it was not until the beginning of the next millennium that the professional conversations of lawyers, philosophers, and theologians began to converge, all of which created a discursive environment within which the notions of property, natural law, and personal authority could be reshaped.

The story of how all this happened is actually quite dramatic. In 1070, a copy of Justinian's above-mentioned *Digest* somehow surfaced after being lost for nearly half a millennium. It found its way to the famous law school of Bologna, where it was examined and discussed in great detail by generations of students and professors of both canon law and secular law. For the first time, medieval legal scholars and practitioners could read the actual words of the great Roman jurists of the late Republic and Principate, and could appreciate the power and coherence of the Romans' best legal discourse. Of particular relevance for the medieval lawyers were the Roman jurists' treatment of three issues: (1) property as a primitive *pre-legal fact,* (2) property transfer as a personal *pre-legal agreement* or *actio* between private individuals, and (3) the profound *discrepancy* between the early concept of *dominium* as a primitive fact (in the Republic and early part of the Classical period) and the later idea that Roman property owners were really just high profile leaseholders who had been allowed to participate in the Emperor's universal *dominium*. It was from such rediscovered texts that the lawyers and scholars of the 11th and 12th centuries were able to construct their own conceptions of ownership and then read them back into early patristic debates about whether there was private property in the Garden of Eden.

By the end of the Roman Empire, Christianity had been flourishing intellectually and socially for over two centuries. However, as in most growth spurts Christendom had serious growing pains, not the least of which was its own confusion about the legal procedures for settling property claims between individuals as well as about the nature of ownership in general. In the long era of vulgar law, the resolution of ownership issues had remained very *ad hoc,* in church tribunals as well as in secular courts. If a manifestly deserving person such as a poor widow did not have clear title to a piece of property, a sympathetic judge might arbitrarily rule that she could continue to occupy the property (i.e., have *possessio*) for thirty years, after which time full ownership could be awarded to her because the previous owner no longer had legal *dominium*. In other cases, such as a sale that had been made under ambiguous terms, the judge might base his ruling on what he perceived to be the presence or absence of an appropriate intention or *animo* on the part of the seller, which functioned in a quasi-sacramental way to transform the physical exchange of property (i.e., the actual delivery of the goods in question or bodily occupation of the house or land) into a non-physical but nonetheless real fact, namely the fact of a change of ownership.

Such ad hoc legal reasoning seems strange today, but when it was used in courts that had been influenced or even established by the church, it had a prima facie authority that was seldom questioned. Indeed, there were many cases of disputed possession that directly involved church property, such as whether a bishop who at the request of the local community had moved into the diocesan chancery had some sort of squatter's priority over another bishop who had been appointed to take over the diocese but had not yet arrived. To put it gently, in the early Middle Ages the discourse of conflict resolution in clerical as well as secular affairs was itself a work in progress, especially when property was involved. Even so, Christianity had introduced into the mix a new element that in retrospect had been conspicuous by its absence in Roman law.

This element was the Christian idea that each person had a direct relationship to a deity who was not only the Supreme Being but also a loving father. In this scheme of things, everyone possessed what one twentieth century theologian has called an "alien dignity," which is to say a dignity in the eyes of the divine Other.[32] Looking back, it seems almost inevitable that as the old Roman legal system became combined with Christian suppositions about everyone's personal relationship to God, the idea of *jus* would morph from a legal rule into a personal right. And so it did, but slowly and with great subtlety. The concept of alien dignity was usually filtered through other more or less hierarchical models, according to which legitimate authorities were understood as holding rights either directly (as God's representatives) or indirectly (by possessing rights inherent in the offices they held).[33]

But where exactly did this concept come from? Was it a spinoff from the new interest on the part of tenth and eleventh century theologians in St. Paul's doctrine of the Mystical Body? Perhaps. This seems to be Brian Tierney's view,[34] but the medieval historian Heinrich Rommen has proposed a more worldly explanation, namely that it was self-interested economic and political pressure groups, not theologians, philosophers, or legal theorists, who created the new discourse or at least dramatically extended the range of its central concepts of rights and liberties to new sectors and levels of society.[35] Be that as it may, it is clear that well before the intellectuals began constructing a new philosophical model of rights as powers that people have, kings and feudal lords in "the real world" had been granting new social and economic immunities and privileges not only to neighboring towns but also to professional associations such as guilds and the legal profession, as well as to individuals such as merchants, travelers, and pilgrims.

Feudal Structures and Property Rights

Until a just few decades ago, historians routinely gathered medieval social structures under the umbrella label of "feudalism," but that term is now considered grossly misleading.[36] The stereotype of a powerful lord defended by his devoted vassal knights, with serfs happily at work on manors that the knights had received as fiefs for their loyal service, is a poetic trope, not a hard historical fact. Its gauzy portrayal of medieval power structures ignores the great complexity of the military and agricultural arrangements of that time as well as the many individuals who tilled their own soil, bought and sold merchandise, or drifted into self-governing towns where they labored as smiths and innkeepers or perhaps as thieves and beggars. It certainly leaves out the tension between religious and secular authorities, as well as the people's deep respect for the unknown, a respect not only for the invisible apparatus of medieval Catholicism such as grace and the sacraments but also for the essentially secular notion of rights as moral powers or forces.[37]

It would be a mistake, though, simply to abandon the concept of feudal structures, especially when discussing complex property issues. Although they formed only part of a larger social picture, feudal relations based on personal commitment and loyalty did indeed exist, and in many though perhaps not most cases there were genuine bonds of fidelity between lords and vassals that went beyond the simple landlord-tenant or master-servant relationships. Even though the rights vocabulary had not yet been developed, in actual practice existing lord-vassal relationships included much of what we now call reciprocal rights and duties. What is most important here, though, is that the reciprocity that defined the early, unromanticized version of the feudal relationship was carried over to new political and social contexts, as when the rights-like privileges were extended to town folk, merchant guilds, wandering minstrels, apothecaries, and others, as well as to the towns themselves. In an early essay aptly entitled "The Genealogy of Natural Rights," the above-mentioned Heinrich Rommen has traced the development of "liberties, franchises, immunities and privileges" from earlier arrangements made by townfolk (burghers), including the merchant and artisan guilds, with feudal overlords and kings who needed the financial support of the new "free cities."[38]

In short, the feudal conception of property as a fief was clearly a new model of ownership, profoundly different from the Stoics' dialectical model of property as self-realization. It was equally different from the early Romans' notion of pre-legal appropriation by conquest, cultivation, or first discovery, and the later Romans' notion of imperial dominion in which—despite their legally inferior status —secondary owners had what for all practical purposes was full authority to sell or rent the land whenever and to whomever they chose.

However, the feudal arrangement was not the only medieval conception of ownership. As Levy has shown,[39] there were also other models of ownership in play during the Middle Ages. An especially interesting one was that of properties acquired as *gifts* (many if not most of which were bequests to the Church or its monasteries). In this model there were no "pure" gifts: there was always some implicit *quid pro quo* involving either a reciprocal gift or some other sort of expectation on the part of the donors, their family members, or others who had some sort of dependency relationship with the donor. This meant that the recipients' legal ownership depended on the continuation of an original relationship with the donor (which meant in turn that in some sense the original owner-donor retained certain conditional rights in the property *even after it had been transferred to a third owner*). The best illustration of this complex model is probably the contrast between unconditional dominion and the always-conditional fief. At some point (probably in the early 1200's), the original Roman Republican assumption that property owners enjoyed full, exclusive dominion was back, having replaced the Dominate's idea that ordinary ownership was only some sort of proxy participation in the Emperor's "real" dominion. However, since other ownership patterns were still in play, there was an ongoing need for civil and church courts to sort things out.

A good example of the legal complexity of property ownership in the 11th and 12th centuries is what might be called the problem of overlapping ownership. A case in point arose when the prestigious monastery of Cluny agreed to exchange a parcel of land for a different, somewhat distant piece of property owned by a private individual. Unfortunately for that other owner, the parcel he received in the exchange was originally a gift to the abbey, and so it then reverted to the original owners or, more exactly, to their descendants, who by then made up four distinct family groups. After two and a half decades (1014-1039) of litigation, the case was finally settled in favor of the descendants, presumably leaving all parties feeling that regardless of the outcome, the procedures themselves had (to put it mildly) left much to be desired.

The Canonists' Breakthrough

The Cluny example was only one of many disputes over property and related issues such as the rights of the poor, grounds for divorce, inheritance issues, and even a lord's right to erect a gallows on his estate. During the High Middle Ages (c. 1001-1300), the language of personal rights—especially property rights—expanded and became increasingly sophisticated. We have just seen in the Cluny example some of the complexities of medieval property ownership, and we can easily imagine the frustration that must have been felt by all concerned owing to the absence of a distinctive, institutionalized form of discourse that would provide a moral anchor for the rapidly expanding set of political and social privileges and immunities. However, on the horizon was a new form of rights talk that would include not only property rights (the Stoics' dialectical account of ownership was apparently far too abstract for the Romans, including Cicero, even though he cited it) but also economic rights, such as the right to subsistence, and personal rights, such as the right to marry—and of course the right to life itself. In short, the terms *jus* and *jura* came to denote active powers as well as objective laws and standards. The first recorded instances of this new usage were the scholarly supplements to the compendium of canon law that had been assembled in Bologna by the canon law scholar Johannes Gratian, who was probably born in the early 1100's and probably died around either 1150 or 1160.[40] His great work was the oddly but accurately titled *Concordia Discordantium Canonum* (A Concord of Discordant Canons) or more simply, the *Decretum.*

In its first edition or "recension," Gratian had catalogued and tried to reconcile conflicting papal decrees, since the wounds of the harsh two-century (c. 850-1050) struggle for dominance between emperors and popes were still healing. However, in the process of sorting out this mass of material, he also commented on a huge number of legal, scriptural, theological, and other important texts that had to do with relationships between secular law, church law, and the scriptures. It was followed several years later by a second recension, probably assembled by other scholars in the middle or late 1150s,[41] which included additional primary texts such as scriptural quotations and—of special import here—scholarly commentaries or "glosses" that other compilers or "glossators" had created from authoritative documents such as the early patristic discussions of whether there was property *(dominium)* in the Garden of Eden. (The prevailing view on that issue was negative in spite of scriptural texts to the contrary, such as Psalm 8:6 as well as Genesis 1:26-28.) To these older commentaries the glossators added newer glosses written by themselves or their contemporaries, which were collected either in the second recension of the *Decretum* or in a separate commentary called *The Ordinary Gloss,* or else were discussed in a commentator's own self-titled glossary (e.g., Huguccio of Pisa's magisterial *Summa Decretorium,* c. 1190). In doing so, they introduced a new paradigm of rights as *powers,* which is to say as attributes of human beings that enabled ordinary people to make claims on others not because of some special authority they had as office holders or heads of families, or from some transcendent law that everyone must follow, but rather because of their own newly recognized legal, moral, and religious entitlements.

In this respect the glossators were reinventing some of the discursive practices of the Roman jurists of the late Republic and early Empire, who had always been careful to frame their court exchanges in terms of legal precedents rather than abstract, theory-based rules. Like the classical jurists and rhetors, the medieval glossators apparently recognized that even the most theoretical discourse is interactive in the sense that its speakers or authors are always systematically packaging their thoughts in anticipation of responses and commentaries by others.

This dialogical feature was the hallmark of all medieval scholars, whose academic training always began with the study of the arts of rhetoric and dialectics. Like the educational curriculum of ancient Rome, its focus was on Plato's dialogues and Aristotle's *Topics, Rhetoric,* and other works. Similar versions of this method had been used in the 6th century by Boethius (480-c. 524) and in Gratian's own time by two of his most important, slightly older contemporaries, namely the theologian Peter Abelard (1079-1142) and the scripture exegete Peter Lombard (1096-1164). Using this venerable back-and-forth approach, other canonists began to develop their own commentaries on the *Decretum*, and in the process incubated the new and rapidly developing notion of subjective rights. Although rather labor intensive, the glossing procedure itself is easy to describe. A glossator first sorted out several well-documented statements by established authorities on either side of a central thesis and then showed how those seemingly incompatible or "discordant" statements could be reconciled.[42] To do this, he needed to sort out the different uses of the term *jus natural,* which often required considerable ingenuity on his part. The glossators' collective output of this exegetical technique consisted in long lists of subjective meanings for the term *jus natural,* such as Sicard of Cremona's "force or power naturally instilled in man."[43]

And so it came to pass that, as Tierney and other historians have shown, by the middle of the 13th century, canonists and secular legal theorists were regularly using the subjective language of natural *rights*, even though the moral philosophers and theologians were still wedded to the objective classical notion of natural *law*. How their successors in the Late Middle Ages and the Renaissance slowly "got it" is a separate story, too long to tell here. Suffice it to say that one of its earliest appearances in the philosophical and theological literature was in the famous poverty debates of the 14th century, where the notion of private property was expanded to include the idea that, since property ownership was such a deep-seated, profoundly personal feature of human existence, a solemn vow to forego the exercise of this power or right (as some members of the Franciscan order did) was an offering of the most intimate part of one's self to God. Later debates, such as whether the strange indigenous people of the New World had the cognitive or moral capacity to own property, began with the same premise, namely that property, as well as life itself, was a personal right, at least for (with apologies for the pun) "the right people," namely the Europeans.

The Aftermath

I have tried to show that the social and political structures of the 12th century were the breeding ground for a wide variety of rights claims. The breakdown of the Roman legal system and the absence of any systematic philosophical or theological discussion of rights did not prevent popes and emperors, as well as ordinary property owners and others, from making claims and counterclaims in defense of their respective interests. In the course of making those claims, various subjective factors were recognized, some of which had to do with familiar secular and ecclesiastical legal practices and others with more elusive psychological concepts such as volition, consent, intentionality, and free will. Once the *Decretum* created a forum for rights talk, influential canonists and secular legal scholars were quick to use it. The best-known contests about what we now call rights were probably church-versus-state disputes, but similar disputes took place *within* each domain: priests made claims against their bishops, kings defended their authority against nobles or other kings, and so on. The first such contests were held in secular and religious courts where common sense was the final arbiter. However, it was not long before common sense was not enough, at which point the hitherto unanalyzed conception of law as a moral force became an extremely important issue in itself.

It was almost inevitable, therefore, that the relatively conservative and static conceptions of *jus* as objective law that appeared in Gratian's first recension of the *Decretum* (c. 1139) would be challenged by very different, "subjective" conceptions of *jus* as a force, power, or faculty. These challenges appeared in the second recension of the *Decretum* (c. 1155; authors unknown) as well as in many other glosses assembled in that era. The early discussions dealt with accepted authoritative definitions of natural law, but they contained many inconsistencies or simple contradictions. Later glossators were more critical. Like someone who joins a conversation already in progress, they recognized the inconsistencies of the various definitions or descriptions of the *jus naturalis* and, in line with Gratian's original intention to harmonize relevant texts taken from divergent authorities (the "Concord of Discordant Canons"), they tried to reconcile the conflicting texts. In doing so, they opened a whole new line of scholarly discourse, within which what was natural in the notion of natural law was now understood to be our ability as *self-affirming individuals* to recognize the authority we have over our own lives and our righteous power to demand that others respect that authority. However, for unknown reasons (perhaps including a lack of scholarly interest in the whole topic of canon law), until recently the glossators' various "subjective" conceptions of *jus* were ignored not only by medieval philosophers, theologians, and chroniclers but also by nearly all of the twentieth century historians who discussed the emergence of the notion of natural rights.   Until very recently, the standard view of historians and other scholars was that the discussion of moral rights began with the 17th century rights theories of Thomas Hobbes and John Locke, or perhaps with their postmedieval predecessors such as Francisco de Vitoria (1483-1546) and Hugo Grotius (1583-1645). In our own time, a few intellectual historians, typically those with Scholastic backgrounds such as Michel Villet and Richard Tuck, have traced the concept of moral rights back to the 15th century or even to the early 14th century.[44] However, it was not until Brian Tierney's later investigations of the 12th century canonists' accounts of *jus* as a force that rights theorists[45] could recognize what seems (to me at least) to be the real origins of the longstanding subjective conception of rights.

But what exactly happened between Gratian's completion of the first recension of the *Decretum* and the later commentaries of glossators such as Rufinus and Huguccio? What led to the new subjective conception of *jus* as a personal power? My own view here is that since there was no single person or event that triggered the change, the answer to this question probably has something to do with the *conversational character* of the glossators' eclectic methodology. In the first recension, Gratian always used the word *jus* to denote objective legal systems such as canon law, property law, and of course natural law, or else specific laws within those systems. However, his successors were much less strict or, better, much more tolerant of metonomy.[46] The 12th century glossators who contributed to the second recension of the *Decretum*[47] and the authors of the separate commentaries, including those commentaries collectively known as *The Ordinary Gloss,* did not hesitate to use the word *jus* in two very different ways, namely to designate *a subjective right* that every person has and also *an objective legal system* (or the rules it contained).

Furthermore, there was no fixed list of subjective meanings of the word, although it is safe to say that when *jus* was defined by these authors, it was usually identified as some kind of energy or force. Rufinus

(d. 1191), who along with Huguccio (d. 1210) is usually considered the greatest of the late 12th century canonists or glossators, defined *jus* as a "natural force" (which is reminiscent of Cicero's post-Stoic conception of an inborn power or *vis*),[48] and many others followed his lead. For instance, around 1170 the English canonist Odo of Dover defined natural *jus* as "a certain divinely inspired force in man by which he is led to choose what is right and equitable," and other commentators called it a force, a power, and that superior part of the soul known as *synderesis* or (roughly speaking) *conscience*. One of the most open-ended and dialogical explanations of this point is that of Ricardus Angelicus (d. 1237), who declared, "Some say that natural *jus* is free will ... others say that it is charity ... others say that natural *jus* is the superior part of the soul, namely reason.... *We reject none of these*" (my italics).

Years later, the two late medieval philosophers, Ockham and Gerson, and after them the renaissance and early enlightenment philosophers and jurists just mentioned, would develop more systematic, well-structured accounts that linked the conception of *jus* as a personal faculty to our innate capacity to reason. Whether or to what extent other philosophers of their time had also picked up on the glossator's active notion of *jus* is unclear, but there is no doubt that the glossators themselves had arrived much earlier at the idea of a right as something *a person has*. It is unclear, to me at least, exactly why it took the medieval and post-medieval philosophers and theologians so long to catch up with the glossators' earlier shift from a passive sense of *jus* as a rule we should obey to an active sense of *jus* as a power that we may (and usually should) exercise. But that they did catch up should be no surprise. Important conversations often rearrange world views, and that takes time.

Conclusion

My account of rights has been retrospective, but I think that it has important implications for our contemporary rights talk, which is centered on the relatively new notion of *human rights*. The communication theorist Frank Macke once concluded a discussion of group dynamics with a reflection on John Dewey's account of how meanings are constructed or, as Macke put it, how the literate word becomes corporate flesh.[49] His metaphor also fits the story I have tried to tell in these pages about the history of the word *jus* and its cognates, and there is every reason to expect that it will also fit the contemporary conversation about human rights. As that conversation proceeds, we may expect new paradigms and modes of discourse to develop in which the current philosophical conception of human rights, namely as expressions of our common human interests and agency, will also become new "corporate flesh."

Notes

1. Alberto Merlucci, "Collective Action: A Constructivist View," in *Nomads of the Present: Social Movements and Individual Needs in Contemporary Society,* ed. John King and Paul Mier (Philadelphia: Temple University Press, 1989).
2. Ian Shapiro, "Realism in the Study of the History of Ideas," in *History of Political Thought* 3, no. 3 (1982): 537-78, 577. Commenting on this passage, Brian Tierney has noted that it is also necessary to get our history straight—which he claims Shapiro has not done since he "writes as though the world began in the seventeenth century." From Tierney, "The Origins of Natural Rights Language," *History of Political Thought* 10, no. 4 (1989): 616.

3. I say "almost never" because of the important work on this and related topics by the philosopher Rom Harré, especially his relatively recent "An Ontology for Duties and Rights," in *The Psychology of Rights and Duties: Empirical Contributions and Normative Commentaries,* ed. Norman J. Finkel and Fathali M. Moghaddam (Washington, DC: American Psychological Association, 2008), 223-41.

4. Since the original Roman alphabet did not have the letter "J," most classicists and historians write *ius* and *iura* rather than *jus* and *jura*. However, in deference to non-specialist readers, I have used the latter forms throughout, even when quoting texts with the other spelling.

5. The agreement is general but not universal. See Matthew Dickie's vigorous arguments against those who claim that in the works of Homer, Hesiod, and later writers the terms *dike* and its cognates are simply legal or prudential terms "devoid of moral significance" (p. 91), in his "*Dike* as a Moral Term in Homer and Hesiod," *Classical Philology* 73, no. 2 (1978): 91-101.

6. Hesiod, *Works and Days,* l. 228. See *The Works and Days, Theogony, The Shield of Herakles,* trans. Richmond Lattimore (Ann Arbor, MI: University of Michigan Press, 1968), 250-64.

7. The Plato reference is to the *Republic,* 3, ii, and the Sophocles reference is to *Oedipus Rex,* 863-910. The translations are mine.

8. There is still a generation of Roman Catholics who every week heard the priest and server say this prayer in the original Latin. The priest would invite the congregation to give thanks to the Lord *(Gratias agamus Domino Deo nostro),* to which the server or congregation would reply: *Dignum et justum est,* a pleonasm which church missals variously translated as "It is truly right

and just," "It is fitting and right," or more quaintly, "It is meet and just."

9. Fred D. Miller, Jr., *Nature, Justice, and Rights in Aristotle's Politics* (Oxford: Oxford University Press, 1995); for critiques of Miller, see Malcolm Schofield, "Sharing in the Constitution," *The Review of Metaphysics* 49, no. 4 (1996): 831-58, and Michael Pakaluk, "Aristotle On Human Rights," *Ave Maria Law Review* 10, no. 2 (Spring, 2012): 379-86.

10. Historians have based these dates on the death of Alexander the Great in 330 BC and the conquest of Egypt in 30 BC, which is usually identified as the beginning of the Roman Empire.

11. The term is the title of Martha Nussbaum's *The Therapy of Desire* (Princeton, NJ: Princeton University Press, 1966).

12. Cicero's main sources for Stoic teachings were the later Stoics Panaetius of Rhodes (185-109 BC) and the immensely talented Posidonius of Apameia (c. 135-51 BC), whose lectures Cicero attended early in his own career.

13. *Aeneid,* 6.847-853 (my translation).

14. The debate over the concept of private property has continued through the ages, from John Locke's post-Stoic belief that property was an extension of one's deepest self to Pierre-Joseph Proudhon's famous motto that property is theft and, of course, Karl Marx and Friedrich Engel's famous conception of justice as the distribution "from each according to his ability and to each according to his needs."

15. *De Officiis,* I.7.20. Cicero was hardly the first Roman intellectual to assume that ownership or *dominium* was a natural feature of human existence (albeit not a universal one, since slaves, children, and most women could not own property). However, his contribution to the classical Roman discourse on property was indeed

extraordinary, not only because he wrote in a time when politicians such as Julius Caesar and especially Catalina were questioning the power that the wealthy enjoyed over ordinary citizens as well as over the poor, but also because he so clearly articulated the intellectual and historical (i.e., Stoic) roots of the institution of private property itself. Today we have only fragments of the early Stoics' writings, but it is easy to see how they influenced Cicero and his readers. Although not himself a Stoic (he identified himself as a follower of the post-Aristotelian Academy), Cicero's formal use of the Stoics' model of private property reflected—and was reflected by—the republican Romans' everyday discourse about property issues, which rested on the assumption that *dominium* was a pre-legal fact, protected by Roman law but not created by it.

16. A. A. Long, *From Epicurus to Epictetus* (Clarendon Press: Oxford, 2006), 338-59; see also his "Stoic Philosophers on Persons, Property-Ownership and Community," in *Aristotle and After*, ed. R. Sorabji (London: Institute of Classical Studies, University of London, 1997), 13-31.

17. Because the original source of this famous passage is lost, this citation is taken from Cicero's *De Officiis* 3.42, translated by P. G. Walsh as *On Obligations* (Oxford: Oxford University Press, 2001). I do not share the misgivings about Long's use of this famous text that were expressed by Phillip Mitsis in his "The Stoic Origin of Natural Rights," *Topics in Stoic Philosophy,* ed. K. Ierodiakonou (Oxford: Oxford University Press, 1999), 153-77, and "The Stoics on Property and Politics," http://www.as.nyu.edu/docs/io/1394/stoicsproperty-politics.pdf.

18. After the first table was published, the plebeians still had misgivings, and so a second table, with two more codes, was published a year later, mainly specifying

legal procedures but with a final republican flourish that "whatever the people ordain last shall be legally valid."

19. Livy (Titus Livius), *The History of Rome*, 3.34, 3-6 (my translation).

20. A few of the better-known films and television dramas set in the first part of the Empire are *The Robe* (1953); *Demetrius and the Gladiators* (1954); *Caligula* (1979); *I, Claudius* (1901 through 1976); *Quo Vadis* (1901 through 2002); *Nero* (2004); *Centurion* (2010); *The Eagle* (2011); and *Ben Hur* (1907 through 2010). Clearly, one need not be a classics scholar to find this period fascinating.

21. Many historians identify the end of the Principate with the close of Severus Alexander's reign in 235 AD and treat the so-called "crisis period" of the next fifty years as a buffer between the Principate and the Dominate era that followed.

22. Historians generally believe that although the schools were in some important sense founded by Proculus and Masurius Sabinus, they were following the methods of two prominent jurists of the previous generation, Marcus Antistius Labeo (d. c. 11 AD) and Ateius Capito (d. c. 22 AD) respectively.

23. The *Digest* (full title: *Digesta seu Pandectae*) was part of the *Body of Civil Law (Corpus Juris Civilis)*, compiled in Constantinople (530-533) under Justinian I. It was a collection of cases and other jurist writings, mainly from the Principate era. Most of what was recorded were originally private opinions of the jurists of that time or the preceding century. Thanks to Justinian's *Digest*, they were usually considered legally binding precedents in the Eastern Empire and, as we will see below, provided authoritative guidelines for reconstructing the Western legal tradition after the fall of Rome in 476 AD.

24. The standard source for the Romans' shifting conceptions of property is Ernst Levy, *West Roman Vulgar Law: The Law of Property* (Philadelphia: American Philosophical Society, 1951). However, see also Peter Stein, *Roman Law in European History* (Cambridge: Cambridge University Press, 1999). For a sociological-anthropological account of the origins of property, see Charles Létourneau's now dated but nonetheless masterful *Property: Its Origin and Development* (London: Charles Scribner's Sons, 1892), 256-77.

25. For instance, it was now up to the judge himself, not the precedent-oriented jurist, to decide what issues should be addressed in a trial and what evidence would be submitted, including evidence uncovered by the judge's own investigations. This might seem strange to American readers, for whom judges in both civil and criminal cases are usually impartial referees (our adversary system), but not to Europeans, who are used to the so-called inquisitorial system in which a *juge d'instruction* is directly involved in the investigation.

26. For instance, a *colonus* was legally bound to the land he worked on, as was his first son. However, this new rule did not prevent many *coloni* from quietly relocating to outlying regions, where they were unknown and often became independent landowners themselves.

27. Stein, *Roman Law in European History*, 26.

28. A plaque erected in 1895 at England's Rugby School commemorates the exploit of William Webb Ellis in 1823, who "with a fine disregard for the rules of football as played in his time first took the ball in his arms and ran with it, thus originating the distinctive feature of the rugby game." As for the more problematic origins of courtly love, see Denis de Rougemont, *Love in the Western World,* trans. M. Belgion (New York: Pantheon Books), 1956.

29. "Firmly established" is putting it mildly. For instance, in 390 Ambrose, then bishop of Milan, excommunicated the Emperor himself (Theodosius the Great, r. 379-395) for commanding a massacre at Thessalonica. After Theodosius did penance, Ambrose allowed him back in the church.

30. One unremarked but striking instance of this difference is Ambrose's person-centered use of the word *jus*, which foreshadowed the rights discourse of the medieval Christian theologians. For instance, he exhorted his congregation to share their food because nature has produced "common rights" *(natura igitur jus commune generavit),* although he thought the very idea of private rights was itself a product of greed. See his *De Officiis*, Vol. 1, ed. and trans. Ivor Davidson (Oxford: Oxford University Press, 2002), 194.

31. Historians identify the beginning of the Carolingian period as 800 AD, when Pope Leo III crowned the Frankish king Charlemagne ("Carolinus") as the first Holy Roman Emperor.

32. The phrase "alien dignity" is from Helmut Thielicke, *Modern Faith and Thought* (New York: Eerdmans Publishing, 1990), *passim*.

33. See Walter Ullmann, *The Individual and Society in the Middle Ages* (Baltimore: The Johns Hopkins Press, 1966), 11 ff.

34. See Brian Tierney, "Religion and Rights: A Medieval Perspective," *Journal of Law and Religion* 5, no. 1 (1987): 163-75.

35. Heinrich A. Rommen, "The Genealogy of Natural Rights," *Thought* 29, no. 3 (1954): 403-25, 407.

36. See Elizabeth Brown's now-famous critique of professional historians' use of the term feudalism (the so-called "F-word") in "The Tyranny of a Construct: Feudalism and Historians of Medieval Europe," *The American Historical Review* 79, no. 4 (1974): 1063-88.

See also the important contributions of her distinguished pupil Susan Reynolds, especially *Fiefs and Vassals. The Medieval Evidence Reinterpreted* (Oxford: Oxford University Press, 1994), and *Kingdoms and Communities in Western Europe* (Oxford: Oxford University Press, 1997).

37. Charles Taylor has discussed the medievals' respect for the unknown under the heading of "the age of enchantment," especially in his *A Secular Age* (Cambridge: Harvard University Press, 2007); see also David McPherson, "Re-Enchanting the World: An Interview with Charles Taylor," *Philosophy and Theology* 24, no. 2 (2012): 275-94.

38. Rommen, "The Genealogy of Natural Rights." Rommen also notes that many of the towns that grew up at that time had names like Freiburg, Freistadt, Ville franche, and Villa franca.

39. Levy, *West Roman Vulgar Law*, 21-43, 84-99, 127-49. See also Barbara Rosenwein, *To Be the Neighbor of St. Peter: The Social Meaning of Cluny's Property,* 909-949 (Cornell University Press: Ithaca, New York, 1989), 109-43.

40. See Kenneth Pennington, "The Biography of Gratian, the Father of Canon Law," *Villanova Law Review* 59, no. 4 (2014): 679-706.

41. Anders Winroth argues for this view in *The Making of Gratian's Decretum* (Cambridge: Cambridge University Press, 2000). However, not all agree. See Pennington, "The Biography of Gratian."

42. Although the first Christian dialectician was Boethius, the dialectical method will be familiar to many readers because of the use Thomas Aquinas made of it in the 13th century in his *Summa Theologicae*.

43. The quotation is from Sicard of Cremona's *Summa Canonum* (1179-1181), as cited in Tierney, *Idea of Natural Rights,* 60.

44. Ockham's *Opus Nonaginta Dierum* was probably finished in 1333. Michel Villey has argued that Ockham was the first natural rights theorist; see M. Villet, *Le Droit et les Droits de l'homme* (Paris, Presses Universitaires de France, 1983). In contrast, Richard Tuck has argued that the title of first natural rights theorist belongs to Jean Gerson, whose *De Vita Spirituali Animae* appeared in 1402; see R. Tuck, *Natural Rights Theories* (Cambridge: Cambridge University Press, 1979).

45. Or at least most rights theorists. See Alasdair MacIntyre's famous dismissal of the whole notion of moral rights, namely that "there are no such rights, and belief in them is one with belief in witches and in unicorns," in his *After Virtue: A Study in Moral Theory* (South Bend, IN: Notre Dame Press, 1981), 65.

46. A useful, albeit somewhat later, example of metonymy is the history of the word "want," which according to *The Oxford English Dictionary* originally (in the 1300's) meant an objective lack of something desirable, then that which was lacking, and only much later (c. 1700) the desire itself.

47. Gratian apparently finished the first recension in 1139 or slightly later. The second recension was probably finished in the 1150's, but not by Gratian himself. See Anders Winroth, *The Making of Gratians' Decretum* (Cambridge: Cambridge University Press, 2000), 138, 144-45.

48. "[T]he origin of law appears to be from nature, since there is a law of nature which we have, not from opinion but from a kind of inborn power." Cicero, *De Legibus*, 1.6,18 (my translation).

49. Frank Macke, "Group Dynamics and Culture," *Listening: Journal of Communication Ethics, Religion, and Culture* 48, no. 2 (2013): 149-64, 160. See also John Dewey, *How We Think* (New York: D.C. Heath, 2010).

About the Authors

Michelle J. Bellino is Assistant Professor of Educational Studies at the University of Michigan School of Education. Her research centers on the intersection of history education and youth civic development, particularly in contexts of armed conflict and their aftermath. She is also actively exploring the role of the educational sector as a mechanism of transitional justice in emergent democracies. Her work has been featured in numerous journals and several collections on history education and related topics. Contact information: michelle.bellino@gmail.com.

David T. Ozar is Professor of Philosophy at Loyola University of Chicago as well as Adjunct Professor of Medical Humanities in Loyola's Stritch School of Medicine, a combination which reflects his interest in health care and medical ethics issues as well as more theoretical topics such as metaethics, normative ethics, the history of ethics, and—as a longstanding focus—human rights. He has published several articles and books on human rights and related issues, with article titles such as "Rights: What They Are and Where They Come From," "Justice and a Universal Right to Basic Health Care," and "Do Corporations Have Moral Rights?" He has also done extensive work on the structure of other social systems, especially the professions and their ethics. Contact information: dozar@luc.edu.

Patricia H. Werhane is the Wicklander Chair of Business Ethics Emerita, DePaul University, as well as the Ruffin Professor Emeritus, University of Virginia, and Visiting Senior Research Fellow, St. Thomas University. She is the author or editor of 27 books and over a hundred articles and book chapters. Her latest book is *Obstacles to Ethical Decision-Making,* with Laura Pincus Hartman, Crina Archer, Elaine E. Englehardt and Michael S. Pritchard (Cambridge University Press, 2013). Contact information: pwerhane@depaul.edu.

Thomas E. Wren is Professor of Philosophy at Loyola University of Chicago, where he teaches courses in ethics, social philosophy, and social construction theory. His research interests are ethics, moral psychology, and the philosophy of education, as well as the epistemological foundations and historical dimensions of social construction theory. He has published numerous books and articles, the most recent of which is *Conceptions of Culture: What Multicultural Educators Need to Know* (Rowman & Littlefield, 2012). Contact information: twren@luc.edu.

www.ingramcontent.com/pod-product-compliance
Lightning Source LLC
Chambersburg PA
CBHW020613270326

41927CB00005B/307